WHAT'S NEXT?

The *West Wing* Big Book of Superfan Fun!

SCOTT ROBINSON

ISBN 979-8341488519

Author photograph by Joshua Robinson

For Aaron Sorkin

Also by Scott Robinson...

<u>What's Next?</u>
The West Wing Guide to American Democracy
The West Wing Guide to Global Politics
The Quotable West Wing:
        The Wit and Wisdom of the Bartlet White House
The West Wing Ultimate Superfan Trivia Challenge!
The West Wing Big Book of Superfan Fun!
By Those Who Show Up:
        The West Wing Guide to Progressive Action

<u>Red Brains, Blue Brains</u>
The Psychology of MAGA
Authoritarian We Will Go!
One Big Happy Family

<u>They Long to End Democracy</u>
The GOP
The Christian Nationalists
The Oligarchy
Minority Rule on the March (omnibus)

<u>Zero-Sum Freedom</u>
The Problem of Freedom
The Nature of Freedom
The Assault on Freedom
The Path to Freedom
The Future of Freedom
Freedom Confounded
Zero-Sum Freedom: Democracy vs. Oligarchy in the Battle for
Liberty (omnibus)

Table of Contents

Note

The "Best of" chapters were originally presented in *The Quotable West Wing*, by the author.

The Character Quizzes, Who Said That? quizzes and Guest Stars quiz were originally presented in *The West Wing Ultimate Superfan Trivia Challenge!*, by the author.

Introduction

I love *The West Wing*!

I'm in good company. *The West Wing* has a fandom that rivals that of *Star Trek, Game of Thrones* and *Breaking Bad*. As with those shows, fans like us buy the DVD box sets and put the show on endless loop – or we used to, until it started streaming. Some re-watch all seven seasons every few years; some watch it annually; some just never stop at all (I'm somewhere between those last two).

And, as with those other shows, the nerd factor is high; us Wingnuts, as we like to call ourselves, know the names of all the episodes; can quote entire scenes; can rattle off all the appearances of this recurring character or that. The full corpus of the show's cumulative text is a kind of bible to us.

More than that, the show's high ideals, earnestness, and unblinking commitment to the values its characters exude have, for many if not most of us, been an inspiration in the cultivation of our own values and worldview. It's a glowing portrait of the world as it should be, and it guides our votes, our political convictions, and our service.

It's my hope that herein you'll find all kinds of fun – trivia, humor, nerdy obsession, and possibly some provocative thought. Whatever your takeaways, I wish for you at least some happy memories!

STR
July 2024

In the Sorkinverse

We are blessed in our time with a proliferation of universes – alternate realities into which we steal away whenever we like, indulging in adventures not available to us in our banal reality. These can be complete disconnects (Dune, Middle Earth, the Foundation) or variations on a theme (Marvel's multiverse; *Star Trek*'s Mirror Universe). Whatever the case, it's a place that serves up what the real world doesn't.

Aaron Sorkin created, over two decades, a multiverse of his own: alternate realities based on our own world that serve up variations of important and interesting themes of his choosing: service to high ideals; workplace community; friendship; loyalty; moral ambiguity. Across four television series and even more films, Sorkin pushes these themes beyond the familiar into melodramatic high relief, where we must confront them in all their complexity and challenge, buoyed by endearing characters speaking with passion and clarity we here on Real Earth seldom achieve, if ever.

The Sorkinverse starts somewhere around *A Few Good Men*, spreading outward to *The American President* and *Sports Night*, *The West Wing* and *Studio 60 on the Sunset Strip*, then further still to *The Newsroom* and *Molly's Game*.

Those powerful themes flip dark in some corners of the Sorkinverse, where loyalty and friendship yield to exploration of the extremes of jealousy and betrayal - in *Malice*, *The Social Network* and *Steve Jobs*. Then there are the museum pieces – reflections of our world based on real history, where he brings his kaleidoscopic intellectual and emotional lensing to *Charlie Wilson's War* and *Moneyball* and *The Trial of the Chicago 7* and *Being the Ricardos*.

The Sorkinverse is a place so singular, so distinct, so well-integrated, that we want to stay there, once we've seen it up close. Few fans of *The West Wing* are not also fans of *Sports Night* and *Studio 60* and *The Newsroom*; people who adored *The American President* likely also loved *Moneyball* and *Molly's Game*. If you liked *The Social Network*, you almost certainly like *Steve Jobs* just as much.

And if viewers feel this way about the Sorkinverse, the actors who have lived in it feel it that much more. Many are the players who have been tasked with serving up Sorkin's words and breathing life into his characters in not just one many of his stories. In the pages that follow, this fealty will be showcased in nerdy depth, as those players parade for all the world to see their sugary addiction to his speaking his golden dialog and donning the beloved personas of the Sorkinverse inhabitants.

In no other franchise has one creative voice managed to produce such a vast landscape of ideas, characters, relationships, and mission; nor has any other achieved such a seamless continuity and cohesion. We know Sorkin when we hear him, whether we're told it's him or not; no other dialog sounds like Sorkin dialog; no other characters are as simultaneously familiar and fresh as his.

Much is owed this creator, and his multiverse will persist for decades. Those films and television series will always be revered.

And at the center of them all, there will always be that greatest success, the one that speaks for all the others, the one most beloved:

The West Wing.

~TWW~

Though a great many are mentioned, Fidel Castro is the only real-world head of state to be shown in a *West Wing* episode ("Ninety Miles Away").

~TWW~

Real-world heads of state mentioned on *The West Wing*:

- Winston Churchill ("Manchester, Pt. II")
- Adolph Hitler ("The Women of Qumar")
- Benjamin Disraeli ("The Fall's Gonna Kill You")
- Mao Zedong ("The Portland Trip")
- Fidel Castro ("Ninety Miles Away")
- Indira Gandhi ("The Lame Duck Congress")
- Yasser Arafat ("On the Day Before")
- Muammar Gaddafi ("Pilot")
- Idi Amin ("Freedonia")
- Francisco Franco ("The Al Smith Dinner")

A Few Good Men

A stage play by Aaron Sorkin kicked off a multiverse. And that multiverse included a big-bang creative outpouring of stars – young actors who would take their place in the heavens far beyond A Few Good Men – stars that Sorkin himself made very generous use of. □

Most people know *A Few Good Men* as one of Tom Cruise's early star vehicles. The hit 1992 film about a Navy lawyer who finds himself defending two Marines accused of killing a fellow Marine in the course of a dangerous hazing was, at first, a hit Broadway play in 1989. Starring Cruise as Lt. Kaffee, the lawyer, Demi Moore and Kevin Bacon (also Navy lawyers) and Jack Nicholson in one of his most iconic roles as Col. Jessup, the deceased Marine's commander, the film was one of those rare cases of a perfect movie adaptation of a perfect theater piece. □

Aaron Sorkin wrote the original story on cocktail napkins while tending bar at the Palace Theater on Broadway, after his sister (a Navy lawyer herself) told him about a similar hazing gone wrong at Guantanamo Bay. His agent quickly sold both the stage and film rights. □

The first Broadway run starred Tom Hulce (*Amadeus*) as Kaffee, with Clark Gregg in the Kevin Bacon role (the prosecutor). Gregg was the first *AFGM* alumnus, then, to advance in the Sorkin universe, playing billionaire Calvin Trager in *Sports Night* – and, of course, FBI Special Agent Mike Casper on *The West Wing*.[1]

Hulce was replaced by Timothy Busfield, uberjournalist Danny Concannon on *The West Wing* and tech director Cal Shanley on *Studio 60 on the Sunset Strip*, Sorkin's third TV series. Gregg was replaced by Brad Whitford, who later played not only Josh Lyman on the former, but producer Danny Tripp on the the latter. Soon after joining the *AFGM* cast, he took over the role of Kaffee from Busfield.

Josh Malina may be the *AFGM* king, appearing in the original Broadway production as Jessup's aide, a role he reprised in the movie;

---

[1] Cregg would also go on to inhabit another multiverse – Marvel's, where he played SHIELD Agent Phil Coulson.

he went on to play Jeremy Goodwin on *Sports Night* and Will Bailey on *The West Wing*.

The connections don't end there, and they even go in the other direction: in 2005, a revival of *AFGM* was staged at the Theatre Royal Haymarket in London. Starring as Lt. Kaffee was yet another of the Sorkin faithful: Rob Lowe!

~TWW~

Charlie Young, Danny Concannon and Admiral Fitzwallace all make their debut appearances in the same episode – "A Proportional Response".

~TWW~

Some real-world pop/rock on *The West Wing*:

- "In a New York Minute", Don Henley, in "Somebody's Going to Emergency, Somebody's Going to Jail" (the episode title is taken from its lyrics)
- "Brothers in Arms", Dire Straits, in "Two Cathedrals"
- "My Cherie Amour", Stevie Wonder, "Election Day, Pt. II"
- "I Don't Like Mondays", Tori Amos, "20 Hours in America"
- "Learn to Fly", Foo Fighters, "Mr. Willis of Ohio"
- "One Week", Barenaked Ladies, "College Kids"
- "Rock the Boat", Hues Corporation, "Manchester, Pt. I"
- "Resolve", Foo Fighters, "Election Day, Pt. I"
- "Miracle", Foo Fighters, "Election Day, Pt. II"
- "Desire", Ryan Adams, "King Corn"
- "For What It's Worth", Buffalo Springfield, "Isaac and Ishmael"
- "Beautiful Day", U2, "Election Day, Pt. II"
- "A Change is Gonna Come", James Taylor, "A Change is Gonna Come"

The West Wing Dry Run

It's well-known at this point that The West Wing was, as a TV series, conceived totally on the fly. Aaron Sorkin, already bathed in glory for his Broadway play and hit film *A Few Good Men*, as well as the glorious movie *The American President*, was asked to dinner by TV producer John Wells, who had helmed *China Beach* and *ER*.

Sorkin famously didn't realize he was being invited to pitch; he thought it was a social dinner, and he was primed to hear all about the shows Wells was so lauded for producing.

The story is told once again in Melissa Fitzgerald and Mary McCormack's excellent book, *What's Next? A Backstage Pass to The West Wing*.

"Right after I sat down, John said, 'So what do you want to do?' And instead of saying, 'I think there's been a misunderstanding, I don't have an idea for a television series,' which would've been honest, I said, 'I want to do a series about some staffers at the White House.' John just looked at me and said, 'You got a deal.'"

Fitzgerald & McCormack add the detail that just the evening before, Sorkin had been hosting friends in his home and had chatted with screenwriter Akiva Goldsman (*A Beautiful Mind*) in his basement, who had pointed to a poster of *The American President* and said, "You know what would make a good television series? That!"

When Wells asked for an idea, then, Sorkin just blurted out the first one that came to mind, prompted by Goldsman's comment the previous evening.

And, of course, the DNA of *The American President* runs all *The West Wing*, from the concept to the cast to specific episodes. It was, for all practical purposes, *The West Wing* prototype.

And there was plenty to work with. It's also often been told that when Sorkin wrote the screenplay for *TAP*, he generated almost 500 pages – three times what most screenplays require. What didn't make it into the film had ended up in a desk drawer. Sorkin went back to it for material he could use on the new show.

The obvious connections start at the top, with the similarities between *TAP*'s President Andrew Shepherd[2] and *TWW*'s President Jed Bartlet:

- Both are former university professors;
- Both are progressive liberals;
- Shepherd studied under a Nobel Prize-winning economist; Bartlet *is* a Nobel Prize-winning economist;
- Both chose their best friend as their Chief of Staff;
- Both are indecisive at times, requiring a kick in the pants from that CoS to move them to action;
- Neither served in the military;
- Both presidents are *Abu el Banat* – fathers of daughters;
- Both oppose a Constitutional amendment prohibiting flag-burning;
- Both oppose school vouchers, believing first and foremost in public education;
- Both love to school young people in history: Shepherd, his daughter Lucy; and Bartlet, his body man Charlie;
- Both have a Secret Service bodyguard they call "Coop";
- Both have elderly executive secretaries (Mrs. Chapel, Mrs. Landingham);
- Both have their bedrooms casually invaded at all hours by their senior staff;
- Last but not least, both say, "What's next?"

Some *TWW* plots were lifted right out of *TAP* – "A Proportional Response", for instance, a story of terrorist retaliation in which President Bartlet does not understand why his military response to the sneak-attack deaths of American servicemen must be tempered with highly constrained tit-for-tat. *TAP*'s President Andrew Shepherd asks the same question when faced with the same situation.

The American President's plot is driven by two moving parts – President Shepherd's commitment to progressive legislation addressing climate change and gun control (excuse me, crime control). The former is championed by the fictional Global Defense Council,

---

[2] Played perfectly by Michael Douglas.

which resurfaces in "The Drop-In" on *TWW*.

A state dinner is given for the new French President d'Astier in *TAP*; d'Astier is mentioned in *TWW* ("20 Hours in America", "Liftoff").

In *TAP*, President Shepherd wheels and deals in a way that causes his lobbyist girlfriend Sydney Ellen Wade's[3] environmental bill to fail; on *TWW*, Josh Lyman wheels and deals in a way that causes his lobbyist girlfriend Amy Gardner's efforts to curtail marriage incentives to fail (in "Posse Comitatus").

Both have a boss named Leo.

TAP's Lewis Rothschild is bifurcated into Sam Seaborn and Toby Ziegler in *TTW*: Lewis has Sam's eloquence of pen, as well as Toby's disappointment when the President plays it safe.

Andrew Shepherd's press secretary Robin McCall is a tall, smart, opinionated woman; so is Jed Bartlet's CJ Cregg.

TAP's pollster Leon Kodak is the original Joey Lucas.

Andrew Shepherd is baffled, as is Leo McGarry, over the relationship women have with their shoes.

And the cast bleed-over from *The American President* to *The West Wing* is a gusher:

Martin Sheen: Chief of Staff AJ MacInerney in *TAP*; President Bartlet on *TWW*;

Josh Malina: Sydney Ellen Wade's environmental colleague David in *TAP*; Sam Seaborn's successor Will Bailey on *TWW*;

Anna Deavere Smith: press secretary Robin McCall in *TAP*; National Security Advisor Nancy McNally on *TWW*;

Nina Siemaszko: Sydney Ellen Wade's sister Beth in *TAP*; Ellie Bartlet on *TWW*.

Then there are some smaller players who also went from *TAP* to *TWW*:

Ralph Meyering, Jr. played a Sit Room military advisor in *TAP* ("We'll level the building!"); he appeared in *TWW* Sit Room scenes 10 times;

Ron Canada played a reporter in *TAP* ("Is there a Republican who

---

[3] Equally perfectly played by Annette Bening.

can mount a serious challenge, and are you that candidate?"); he played Under Secretary of State Theodore Barrow in 8 episodes of *TWW*;

Thom Barry played the cheerful front-gate security guard who greets Sydney Ellen Wade in *TAP* ("Sydney Ellen Wade of Virginia – knock 'em dead!"). He was New York Congressman Mark Richardson in 3 episodes of *TWW*.

~TWW~

Many are the real-world visitors seen in WestWingWorld!

David Hasselhoff and **Jay Leno** appear as their real selves in "20 Hours in LA"

Penn & Teller entertain at Zoey Bartlet's birthday party (appearing to torch an American flag in the process) in "In the Room"

Yo-Yo Ma performs at the White House in "Noël"

Barenaked Ladies play in "College Kids"

James Taylor does as well in "A Change is Gonna Come"

Crosby, Stills & Nash are heard but not seen in "An Khe"

Forrest Sawyer moderates the contest between Santos and Vinick in "The Debate"

Jon Bon Jovi hitched a ride on the Santos campaign bus in "Welcome to Wherever You Are"

The Foo Fighters performed as themselves in "Election Day, Pt. I and II"

The Staff That Might Have Been

Much of *The West Wing*'s origin story is well known to the Wingnuts – the superfans – who celebrate the show. Part of that story necessarily details the impressive array of actors who auditioned for main roles in the show, but lost out to Martin Sheen, John Spencer, Allison Janney, Richard Schiff and Rob Lowe.

Who were they, and what might the Bartlet White House have looked like if things had gone differently?

"My feeling in casting, and it's shared by Tommy [Schlamme]," Aaron Sorkin told Melissa Fitpatrick and Mary McCormack for their book *What's Next?*, "is sort of like the NFL draft. Just take the best athletes available. Sometimes actors are right or wrong for parts, but mostly you're not gonna go wrong if you just have a real world-class actor in there."

That's what they shot for. That's what they got. In some cases, the actor and the role didn't always fall together immediately.

It is well known to most Wingnuts that the character Jed Bartlet was originally not going to appear all that often on the show – maybe one episode out of every four – to keep the focus on the young staffers. To that end, Sorkin and Schlamme were originally looking for a particular demeanor, rather than a full-service series star.

A big-name actor with gravitas and casual availability would do the trick. Names like James Earl Jones and Sidney Poitier were kicked around; the idea of a female president – maybe Helen Mirren or Jane Fonda – was considered. Jason Robard's name came up. So did the unlikely name of George Steinbrenner, the controversial owner of the New York Yankees.

The boots-on-the-ground auditions included John Cullum, best known on television as Holling Vincoeur on *Northern Exposure*. Veteran actor Hal Holbrook, who later appeared as Assistant Secretary of State Albie Duncan,[4] read for the part.

Martin Sheen, who of course knew Aaron Sorkin from The American President, came to the role by way of his agent, who sent

---

[4] In "Gone Quiet" and "Game On".

him the pilot script. Excited by what he read, and unconcerned that it was not a full-time role, he had a phone call set up with Sorkin, making clear right away that he wanted the part. The only reason Sorkin hadn't offered it to him in the first place, according to *What's Next*, was that he "considered their odds of landing him for Bartlet somewhere between slim and none."

Casting Leo was tricky because the part called for an actor who could come across as a gruff, git-'er-done politico with a map of the world on his face – someone as unlike Martin Sheen's chief of staff in *The American President* as possible. One great prospect who read for the role was Bob Gunton, who played the corrupt warden in *The Shawshank Redemption*. A very surprising and interesting alternative was CCH Pounder, who is both black and female – a *very* different Leo.

Fitzgerald & McCormack (they sound like a buddy detective show) wrote that Aaron Sorkin kept coming back to Tommy Schlamme, saying, "We need someone like John Spencer!" To which Schlamme eventually replied, "What about John Spencer?"

The most famous instance of neck-and-neck competition was certainly for the role of Toby Ziegler.

"We read a lot of people for Toby, and it was a great part," according to casting director John Levey in *What's Next?* "Toby was like the *Peanuts* character Pig-Pen, but followed around by *worry*, instead of a cloud of dust."

"Talk about right for the part," said Levey of Richard Schiff. "He is the embodiment of ambivalence. And that was perfect for Toby, just perfect."

According to *What's Next*, Schiff attended a party in Los Angeles, years after landing the role, and was approached by Eugene Levy, veteran comic actor most lately of *Schitt's Creek* fame.

"I don't know if you're aware of this," he said to Schiff, "but I was the other actor that was up for Toby the day you tested, and I was 100% sure I got the part." Why? "Because I put my ear against the door when you auditioned and I couldn't hear an effing word you said!"

The tricky part of playing CJ Cregg was going to be delivering serious bits of news to reporters across a podium – and sometimes those bits would be funny, but had to be delivered dead-pan. So the actor cast in the part had to be serious-funny.

Allison Janney had just been in the political film *Primary Colors*, where her capacity for the pratfall was on full display, and *American Beauty*, where she'd played the dark and grave role of the haunted, PTSD-ridden wife of Chris Cooper. She wasn't thinking TV roles at the time; she was thinking movies. But when she heard that the CJ Cregg role was for an Aaron Sorkin show, she changed her mind.

"She was so damn funny," John Levey told Fitzgerald & McCormack, "and so smart." And, because it was Sorkin dialog, she had to be fast. "Allison had all three."

Lo and behold, her competition was the same as John Spencer's – CCH Pounder.[5] The two emerged as the finalists for CJ, with Allison winning out for her pratfall capacity (which she displayed up front on a gym treadmill in the pilot episode).

The casting of Josh and Sam must be told together, for reasons that will become clear (this story is almost as legendary as the Richard Schiff/Eugene Levy tale).

Aaron Sorkin and Brad Whitford had known each other from A Few Good Men, as mentioned above. Sorkin reached out to him directly with the pilot script, offering him the role of Josh over the phone.

"Reading the pilot, I was blown away," Whitford told Fiztgerald & McCormack. "I just thought, 'I love this character, I love this guy, I share his politics. We share a personality!'"

He read for the role, pushing to the limit and going over the top – which drew big laughs, but also stirred some doubts in Schlamme and Levey, despite Sorkin's enthusiasm. "He's not funny, he's not sexy," is how Whitford remembers the feedback. He pressed his agent to persist in trying to get him back in the door, to Levey's annoyance.

He finally got back in and read with Moira Kelly (who played Mandy Hampton). Sorkin soon called to tell him he was in, he was cast! But... as Sam.

Whitford was grateful to be cast at all, but felt deeply that the role

---

[5] Her prominence in *The West Wing* auditions process owed to her work for John Wells on *ER*. She went on to guest-star in The West Wing as Deborah O'Leary, the administrations Secretary of Housing and Urban Development, in the episode "Celestial Navigation".

was wrong: he wasn't Sam – he was *Josh!*

Like Allison Janney, Rob Lowe was a creature of the silver screen, not the small screen – and had in fact never done a TV series before. And like Martin Sheen, his involvement in *The West Wing* came by way of a script sent to him by his agent. And like Janney, when he saw that it was a Sorkin script, he perked up.

"Nobody had told me what part to think about when I read it," according to *What's Next* – but he immediately homed in on Sam Seaborn. "There was something about Sam," wrote Fitzgerald & McCormack, "his unbridled passion perhaps, a Kennedy-esque penchant for soaring idealism and great hair – that he connected with, instantly and on a visceral level."

"This is my part and I'm just gonna go in and blow the doors off it for these guys," Lowe remembered.

This time it was Sorkin who hedged. Lowe brought star power to The West Wing, which thrilled the front office, but per the Fitzgerald & McCormack account, Sorkin didn't see that as necessary or appropriate – he wanted a true ensemble.

But when Lowe came in to read, playing the Mallory scene from the pilot, he did indeed blow the doors off the place – even for Sorkin.

"I don't remember the second or third [scenes] because he'd already gotten the part a page into the first," Sorkin remembered, "and I was thinking of stories for a character who has no idea he looks like Rob Lowe."

With Lowe so perfectly suited to Sam and his deal already in the works, Sorkin seized the opportunity to press for Whitford as Josh – as he had originally conceived. That he had capitulated on Lowe may have helped move Schlamme and Levey to be more open-minded about the unfunny, unsexy Whitford. He was Josh, a role he felt he was born to play, and Lowe was Sam – a role *he* felt he was born to play.

Now, just to tie all of this up in a nice, provocative bow, let's consider the following:

So tightly integrated were the characters, as Bartlet's senior staff, that any face among the actors playing them, other than the actors who actually did, would have wrought significant shifts in the chemistry of the group. Imagine, for instance, that Eugene Levy had gotten the role of Toby, but all the other actors were the ones we know.

Picture the One Square Foot of Real Estate scene. Or the Wrath of the Whatever from High Atop the Thing scene.

Now let's go all out: imagine the pilot Break's Over scene, or the I Wasn't Supposed to Take Them Both scene, or the Chili in the Residence scene - with *this cast...*

Hal Holbrook as Jed Bartlet
Bob Gunton as Leo McGarry
CCH Pounder as CJ Cregg
Eugene Levy as Toby Zeigler
Rob Lowe as Josh Lyman
Brad Whitford as Sam Seaborn

~TWW~

Legitimate Dude Sightings

Since *The West Wing*, Martin Sheen has kept very busy in both film and television. Here are some places you can find him:

- Playing Peter Parker's Uncle Ben in *The Amazing Spiderman*;
- In Martin Scorsese's 2006 crime thriller *The Departed*;
- In *The Way*, a film written, directed and produced by his son Emilion Estevez in 2016;
- In *Selma* (2014), a historical drama about the 1965 civil rights march;
- On *Studio 60 on the Sunset Strip*, in an uncredited voice role as a radio host;
- On the streaming comedy *Grace and Frankie*, co-starring with *West Wing* alum Lily Tomlin.

All in the Family

A Few Good Men spawned the original stable of Sorkinverse actors, including Brad Whitford, Josh Malina, Clark Gregg, Timothy Busfield. Gregg advanced to both *Sports Night* and *The West Wing*; Whitford went on to *The West Wing* and *Studio 60*. Malina outdid them all, appearing in *The American President*, *Sports Night*, and *The West Wing*.

And as we've noted above, *The American President* added even more actors who would make repeat appearances in the Sorkinverse: Martin Sheen, Anna Deavere Smith, Josh Malina, Nina Siemaszko, Ralph Meyering, Jr., Ron Canada, and Thom Barry.

But from *Sports Night* on, there were even more:

Felicity Huffman, who played Dana Whitaker in *Sports Night*, appeared as a Congressional staff chief in *The West Wing* episode "The Leadership Breakfast") and played herself in the *Studio 60* pilot;

Matthew Perry, who played Associate White House Counsel Joe Quincy in 3 episodes of *The West Wing*, starred alongside Brad Whitford as Matt Albie in *Studio 60*;

Teri Polo, who played Dan Rydell's love interest Rebecca Wells in *Sports Night*, was Helen Santos in *The West Wing*;

Allison Janney, *The West Wing*'s CJ Cregg, appeared as herself on *Studio 60*;

John Goodman was interim President Glen Allen Walken in a three-episode story arc on *The West Wing*; he then pulled down an Emmy for his turn as Judge Robert Bebe in a two-parter on *Studio 60*;

Janel Maloney, Donna Moss on *The West Wing*, previously played wardrobe assistant Monica Brazelton in an episode of *Sports Night*;

Nina Siemaszko – Beth Wade in *The American President* and Ellie Bartlet on *The West Wing* – appeared as Holly, nanny to Casey McCall's son Charlie, on *Sports Night* in between the other two roles;

Timothy Davis-Reed, who played Chris, one of the studio techs in *Sports Night*, moved over to the White House press room in *The West Wing*, where he played reporter Mark O'Donnell in many episodes, and played Army Lt. Pierce in two episodes of *Studio 60*;

Alanna Ubach was Catherine Brenner, Dan Rydell's publicist on *Sports Night* – and then chastised Sam Seaborn for what she considered sexist remarks to Ainsley Hayes as Celia Walton on *The West Wing*;

John Mahon never appeared on *The West Wing*; but he was the Chairman of the Joint Chiefs in *The American President*, and the more benign George the Front Desk Guy on *Studio 60*.

Lots of back-and-forth between *Sports Night*, *The West Wing* and *Studio 60* going on here; but what about Sorkin's fourth TV series, *The Newsroom*?

John Gallagher, Jr., who played the jilted teenager Tyler in "20 Hours in America" on *The West Wing*, went on to star as Jim Harper in *The Newsroom*;

Adam Arkin, Dr. Stanley Keyworth on *The West Wing*, guest-starred as a Republican campaign operative on *The Newsroom*;

Mary McCormack, *The West Wing*'s Kate Harper, went on to play Molly the FBI agent in two episodes of *The Newsroom*;

Joanna Gleason was Leo McGarry's attorney (and love interest) Jordan Kendall on *The West Wing*, then Charlie Skinner's widow on *The Newsroom*;

Philip Baker Hall played Sen. Matt Hunt on *The West Wing*, and was then Congressman Bryce Delaney, turned out by the Tea Party on *The Newsroom*, where Will McAvoy interviewed him.

Finally, in one of the most fun facts of the Sorkinverse players, two stars of *The West Wing* – Martin Sheen and Lily Tomlin – paired up with two stars from *The Newsroom* – Jane Fonda and Sam Waterston – to collectively star in *Grace and Frankie*; not a Sorkin show, but certainly a Sorkin legacy!

~TWW~

Most actual US Presidents, from Nixon on back, are explicitly mentioned on *The West Wing*:[6]

George Washington, "Six Meetings Before Lunch", "H. Con-172"
John Adams, "The Leadership Breakfast", "Jefferson Lives"
Thomas Jefferson, "Jefferson Lives", "Privateers"
James Madison, "Let Bartlet Be Bartlet"
James Monroe, "The Leadership Breakfast"
John Quincy Adams, "The US Poet Laureate"
Andrew Jackson, "The Crackpots and These Women"
James K. Polk, "The Fall's Gonna Kill You"
Franklin Pierce, "The Dogs of War"
James Buchanon, "Night Five"
Abraham Lincoln, "The Debate"
Andrew Johnson, "Six Meetings Before Lunch"
Ulysses S. Grant, "Pilot", "Enemies"
Rutherford B. Hayes, "Night Five"
Benjamin Harrison, "The Leadership Breakfast"
William McKinley, "The Black Vera Wang"
Theodore Roosevelt, "Pilot", "Lies, Damn Lies and Statistics"
William Howard Taft, "Hartsfield's Landing"
Woodrow Wilson, "Noël", "Bartlet for America"
Warren G. Harding, "Guns Not Butter"
Calvin Coolidge, "The Benign Prerogative"
Herbert Hoover, "20 Hours in America, Pt. I", "Requiem"
Franklin D. Roosevelt, "Pilot", "Bad Moon Rising"
Harry Truman, "The State Dinner", "The Dogs of War"
Dwight D. Eisenhower, "Pilot", "Arctic Radar"
John F. Kennedy, "7A WF 83429", "Tomorrow"
Lyndon B. Johnson, "Five Votes Down"
Richard Nixon, "Six Meetings Before Lunch", "17 People"

---

[6] Episode references are incomplete here; there are far too many to list!

Critiquing the Bartlet Presidency:
Thumbs Up!

How would the Bartlet Presidency have been assessed, if it had been real? Various critics have written such assessments, measuring Jed Bartlet by real-world executive standards, with interesting results.

On the positive side, there are the banner accomplishments. President Bartlet appointed the Supreme Court's first Hispanic associate justice, Roberto Mendoza – a progressive liberal, an accomplishment in itself ("The Short List"). He also appointed the first female Supreme Court justice, the liberal Evelyn Baker Lang. ("The Supremes").

He negotiated a peace between Israel and Palestine, a feat that many real-world leaders still doubt can ever be possible – and managed to wrangle at least an adequate amount of international support. ("The Birnam Wood").

He prioritized job creation and education, making moderate gains in each, and brought his economist instincts to bear with a neoliberal focus, promoting free-market approaches to a national economy that was on-again, off-again throughout his presidency – but at one point saw six straight quarters of economic growth (mentioned in "Night Five"), though he lamented his failure to balance the federal budget.

He brokered a settlement between India and Pakistan when hostilities erupted in Kashmir. He implemented a controversial but morally laudable doctrine of humanitarian intervention, announcing it in the State of the Union as he deployed troops to the Equatorial Republic of Kundu to halt a genocide ("Inauguration: Over There"). With his intelligence team, he prevented a terrorist attack on the Golden Gate Bridge ("The Black Vera Wang").

His other international accomplishments include negotiations with North Korea over their nuclear development program, as well as summits with both Russian and China.

Officially, he made progress in election reform by appointing his own commissioners to the FEC; unofficially, his administration accomplished a facilitation of social security reform, uniting Democratic and Republican congressmen in common cause.

Analyzed through the Greenstein typology of leadership qualities, President Bartlet does well in every category, according to a study by Marjory Madeline Zuk of Bucknell University. The key strengths displayed were in organizational capacity and public communication, the former exemplified by his competent and well-integrated executive staff, with whom he actively cultivated a sense of mutual reliance and familial community, the second demonstrated in his formidable command of oratory.

His moral depth is made clear in the anguish he feels when taking drastic but necessary action to protect the country, as in the assassination of Abdul Shareef ("Posse Comitatus"), as well as his resistance to military retaliation – even under tremendous public and Congressional pressure, not to mention his own chief of staff – in response to fatal Palestinian attacks on US congressmen and his friend Percy Fitzwallace, the former Chairman of the Joint Chiefs ("Gaza", "Memorial Day").

He brought considerable intelligence and philosophical insight to the office, displaying an admirable capacity to carry on multiple dialogs at once in high-pressure situations calling for innovative, decisive response ("Hartsfield's Landing"). His emotional authenticity was evident in both his professional demeanor, as when loss of US military lives left him in a rage ("The War at Home"), and in his personal relationships with staff, as with his body man Charlie Young ("The Indians in the Lobby").

He was a leader of genuine empathy, evidenced in his overt commitment to healthcare and education.

The Bartlet Presidency can serve as an authentication of the ethical value of progressive ideals, manifested with intelligence, justice, and compassion.

~TWW~

In "The Crackpots and These Women", Josh has a therapist named Stanley. A year later, in "Noël", Josh has migrated to a new therapist – also named Stanley.

The Top 12 Jed Bartlet Moments

Every *West Wing* character shines, over and over. They were built that way, of course; the idea was to create a group of people who were competent, committed, flawed, and admirable. And over the course of seven years, they each gave us plenty of those shining moments.

Let's start at the top...

"Get your fat asses out of my White House!"

The Mary Marsh Incident was definitive for Josh, of course; he learned the hard way, in the pilot episode, the boundaries his position as representative of the President imposed, that to be glib and insulting on national television toward people who don't share his worldview is maybe not the best way to direct public respect and engagement toward his boss.

But his boss has his own notions of respect and engagement, and the exchange in the Mural Room with Marsh and two of her Evangelical cohorts tees him up to dish out a lesson, as he berates the Rev. Al Caldwell for failing to admonish religious extremism. Josh had served up a dose of righteous bluntness to a hypocrite, and paid a price; Jed Bartlet reminded Josh of boundaries, but laid down one of his own to Marsh, et al – *practice what you preach, or your voice isn't welcome here.*

"Just be wrong! Just stand there in your wrongness and be wrong!"

The President and the First Lady were just Jed and Abbey, married 30 years, before he assumed office – and, like any married couple, have their moments of profound disagreement.

It's one thing to have those moments in the privacy of the residence, but when one erupts in the Oval Office – as it does in "The White House Pro-Am" – the moment gains both gravity and levity. On the one hand, a mistake on the First Lady's part can have an unfortunate impact on White House messaging; on the other, Abbey is married to an egocentric, insufferable know-it-all who has to have the final word. So when she concedes her mistake, and he rushes to keep her from adding a caveat, we see both the side-by-side depth of their personalities and – beyond his own ego – Jed's unwitting acknowledgment of his wife's benign power in their partnership.

"If you ever, ever lie – you're finished with me, understand?"

In this sober, dead-serious moment (in "Bad Moon Rising") between Jed Bartlet and Charlie, we hear an admonition that has many layers. The President is about to be taken to the woodshed by multiple investigations into the scandal of his MS deception, and Charlie will be called upon to testify. This exchange is honest, pragmatically prudent, emotionally vulnerable, and paternally protective: Jed comes off as a bit patriarchal, in the mold of his own father, but the threat he lays down is an act of bomb-on-the-grenade vigilance: he'll do anything he possibly can to ensure that Charlie is not hurt by what he's done.

"You're a son of a bitch, you know that?"

Mrs. Landingham's sudden and senseless death in "18th and Potomac" rattles Jed Bartlet deeply, but the truth is, he was rattled already: the disclosure of his multiple sclerosis and the ensuing backlash is the worst of it, but before that, he was struggling with the reality that his administration had been, thus far, largely ineffectual.

His confrontation of God immediately following Mrs. Landingham's funeral, in "Two Cathedrals", represents a confrontation with himself, as his insecurity collides with his indignation and he wrestles with whether he wants to carry on at all.

"That was awfully nice of you..."

Leo is put through the ringer in "Bartlet for America", as their political opponents attempt to pressure Jed Bartlet by leaning hard on his best friend and right-hand man. We see into their past, sharing the moment in which Leo convinced Jed to run for President – and become aware of the love that lived in that moment. When Jed returns the *Bartlet for America* napkin that had been Leo's touchstone, thanking him for that love, Leo begins to weep.

> *"Before I go, please let me just say this...*
> *I'm seriously thinking about getting a dog."*

The President's sense of humor is brainy and ironic – and, for some, an acquired taste ("Sir, you and I enjoy your funny jokes, but Idaho, you know, not so much!") – but Jed Bartlet can be funnier still when he isn't trying at all. Accidentally overdosed for back pain on Vicodin and Percocet, he wanders into the Oval Office (in "Five Votes Down") as loopy as we ever get to see him, and has a brief, hilarious exchange with the staff that leaves them both amused and alarmed. It's the one moment in the series when we get to see him utterly disinhibited, revealing both his affection for the people around him and his contrasting longing for the domesticity his responsibilities are obstructing.

> *"I'm Joe Betherson...ton. That's one 't',*
> *and with an 'h' in there."*

Ah, the Butterball Hotline scene! – one of the show's shrewdest comedic moments.[7] As Jed Bartlet revels in the delightful Americana of a modern world that serves up free turkey-cooking advice by phone on demand, we get to laugh, not only at his incapacity for improvising fake names, but at his ivory-tower cultural ineptitude: how can you claim to be "folksy" if you don't know there's a Butterball Hotline?

> *"In the future, if you're wondering – 'Crime – boy, I don't know'*
> *is when I decided to kick your ass!"*

Randomly encountering his Republican opponent Rob Ritchie in the lounge of a Broadway theater on a night fraught with stress, Jed

---

[7] In "The Indians in the Lobby".

Bartlet is confronted with his own public image, in Ritchie's casual contempt and patronizing condescension. This has to rankle him, as he's already been wrestling with guilt, self-doubt and the consequences of his mistakes for months.

But the exchange with Ritchie in "Posse Comitatus" reminds him what's at stake: an agenda packed with badly-needed initiatives that will go south, waved away by a looming and dismissive right-wing indifference, if his administration's opponents manage to supplant him. He rallies, and with this pronouncement, he locates his resolve: Governor Ritchie, it's on...

> *"I'm going to stay right here,*
> *as long as the radio works, okay?"*

A US carrier fleet has sailed right into a hurricane and is besieged, in "The State Dinner" – and a line between the White House and one of the endangered ships, the *USS Hickory* (a small tender ship) is established. As a state dinner proceeds elsewhere in the White House, Jed Bartlet talks to a young radioman aboard the ship, which is being tossed asunder. The sailor describes the tumult of the storm, the darkness, the waves, the fire aboard ship, and the possibility of the carrier overrunning it, as the President listens and tries to comfort him in the moments before his death.

> *"This was made for my family by a Boston silversmith named*
> *Paul Revere."*

The love between Jed Bartlet and his body man, Charlie Young, can only be described as father-and-son. Their bond is evident in episode after episode, with Charlie's devotion to the President reciprocated as paternal affection. In "The Indians in the Lobby", he expresses that affection in a singular way – handing down a priceless family heirloom as a symbol of his respect and admiration for Charlie.

> *"I was wrong! I was just... I was wrong!"*

Faced with Congressional censure, weary from the toll of public turmoil over his MS revelation, Jed Bartlet sits with Leo and tells him of a decision he's made: while he may have implored his wife to stand there in her wrongness and be wrong, he realizes he must do the same, and accept the censure. Take responsibility for what he and his best friend both know, in their deepest hearts, was a violation of the public trust. This moment in "H. Con – 172" reveals a man of honesty, integrity, and – a trait we might doubt from time to time – humility.

> *"If you expect anything different from the President of the United States, I suggest you vote for somebody else."*

Josh Lyman is sitting in a Nashua VFW watching the locals eat chicken and green Jell-O, as Governor Jed Bartlet answers a challenging question from a constituent about his controversial dairy bill.[8] The scene is noteworthy for a number of reasons, not the least of which is that it's the first time in WestWingWorld that Josh Lyman and Toby Ziegler are in the same room together (although neither realizes it).

The second-most noteworthy aspect is the nature of Jed's answer to the question, why did he vote against the bill?

"One in five children live in the most abject, dangerous, hopeless, backbreaking, gut wrenching, poverty - one in five, and they're *children*. If fidelity to freedom and democracy is the code of our civic religion, then surely the code of our humanity is faithful service to that unwritten commandment that says, 'We shall give our children better than we ourselves had!' I voted against the bill 'cause I didn't want it to be hard for people to buy milk."

The most noteworthy aspect of the scene is Jed's forthrightness in the expression of his values – political cost be damned! So impressed is Josh that he not only joins the campaign; he immediately recruits his old friend Sam.

---

[8] A flashback, in "In the Shadow of Two Gunmen, Pt. I".

The Best of Jed Bartlet

"Before I go, please let me just say this: I'm seriously thinking about getting a dog."

~"Five Votes Down" (S1/E4)

"There, you see how benevolent I can be, when everyone does what I tell them to do?"

~"The Crackpots and These Women" (S1/E5)

"Bless me, Father, for I have sinned..."

~"Take This Sabbath Day" (S1/E14)

"All kinds of things in California, Zoey. You've got your smog, your freeway shootings, brush fires, mudslides. Plus, apparently, there's a mad rash of flag burning going on, and you don't want a piece of that."

~"20 Hours in LA" (S1/E16)

"Wiseass all you want, but you're coming of age in the 21st century - a century in which I promise you mathematics is going to play a starring role. On the other hand, I would definitely put my shoulder into Intro to Cinema. Intro to Cinema's what got me where I am today."

~"The White House Pro Am" (S1/E17)

"Just be wrong! Just stand there in your wrongness and be wrong, and get used to it!"

~"The White House Pro Am" (S1/E17)

"When I sleep, I dream about a great discussion with experts and ideas and diction and energy and honesty. And when I wake up, I think, 'I can sell that.'"

~"Mandatory Minimums" (S1/E20)

"It's actually 607 small islands in the South Pacific. Interestingly, while its total land mass is only 270 square miles, it occupies more than a million square miles of the Pacific Ocean. Population is 127,000 and the U.S. Embassy is located in the state of Pohnpei and not, as many people believe, on the island of Yap."

~"Lies, Damn Lies and Statistics" (S1/E21)

"Decisions are made by those who show up!"

~"What Kind of Day Has It Been?" (S1/E22)

"Today, for the first time in history, one in five Americans living in poverty are children. One in five children live in the most abject, dangerous, hopeless, backbreaking, gut-wrenching, poverty, one in five, and they're children. If fidelity to freedom and democracy is the code of our civic religion, then surely, the code of our humanity is faithful service to that unwritten commandment that says, 'We shall give our children better than we ourselves had.'

"I voted against the bill 'cause I didn't want it to be hard for people to buy milk. I stopped some money from flowing into your pocket. If that angers you, if you resent me, I completely respect that, but if you expect anything different from the President of the United States, I suggest you vote for somebody else."

~"In the Shadow of Two Gunmen" (S2/E1)

"Tonight, what began on the commons in Concord, Massachusetts, as an alliance of farmers and workers, of cobbles man and tinsmiths, of statesmen and students, of mothers and wives, of men and boys, lives two centuries later as America! My name is Josiah

Bartlet, and I accept your nomination for the Presidency of the United States!"

~"In the Shadow of Two Gunmen, Pt. II" (S2/E2)

"I wanted to ask you a couple of questions while I had you here. I'm interested in selling my youngest daughter into slavery, as sanctioned in Exodus 21:7. Georgetown sophomore, speaks fluent Italian, and always cleared the table when it was her turn. What would a good price for her be? While thinking about that, can I ask another? My chief of staff, Leo McGarry, insists on working on the Sabbath; Exodus 35:2 clearly says he should be put to death. Am I morally obligated to kill him myself, or is it okay to call the police? Here's one that's really important, 'cause we've got a lot of sports fans in this town: touching the skin of a dead pig makes us unclean, Leviticus 11:7. If they promise to wear gloves, can the Washington Redskins still play football? Can Notre Dame? Can West Point? Does the whole town really have to be together to stone my brother Jon for planting different crops side by side? Can I burn my mother in a small family gathering for wearing garments made from two different threads?

"Think about those questions, would you? One last thing, while you may be mistaking this for your monthly meeting of the Ignorant Tight-ass Club, in this building, when the President stands, nobody sits."

~"The Midterms" (S2/E3)

"I'm just gonna sit here and think about plutonium and the things I can do with it."

~"And It's Surely to Their Credit" (S2/E5)

"CJ, I have really no judicial jurisdiction over birds."

~"Shibboleth" (S2/E8)

"I'm victim to my own purity of character."

~"The Drop-In" (S2/E12)

"You're gonna be subpoenaed. I'm confident in your loyalty to me.

I'm confident in your love for me. If you lie to protect me, if you lie just once, if you lie just a little, if you lie 'cause you can't stand what's happening to me and the people making it happen, if you ever, *ever* lie... you're finished with me, you understand?

~"Bad Moon Rising" (S2/E19)

"You're a son-of-a-bitch, you know that? She bought her first new car and you hit her with a drunk driver. What, was that supposed to be funny? 'You can't conceive, nor can I, the appalling strangeness of the mercy of God,' says Graham Greene. I don't know whose ass he was kissing there, 'cause I think you're just vindictive. What was Josh Lyman? A warning shot? That was my son. What did I ever do to yours except praise his glory and praise his name? There's a tropical storm that gaining speed and power. They say we haven't had a storm this bad since you took out the tender ship of mine in the North Atlantic last year... 68 crew! Do you know what a tender ship does? Fixes the other ships! Doesn't even carry guns! Floats around and fixes the other ships and delivers the mail. That's all it can do. *Gratias tibi ago, domine.* Yes, I lied! It was a sin! I've committed many sins! Have I displeased you, you feckless thug? Three-point-eight million new jobs, that wasn't good? Bailed out Mexico, increased foreign trade, 30 million new acres for conservation, put Mendoza on the bench, we're not fighting a war, I've raised three children... That's not enough to buy me out of the doghouse? *Haec credam a deo pio? A deo iusto? A deo scito? Cruciatus in crucem! Tuus in terra servus, nuntius fui; officium perfeci Cruciatus in crucem. Eas in crucem!*

"You get Hoynes!"

~"Two Cathedrals" (S2/E22)

"Words, when spoken out loud for the sake of performance, are music. They have rhythm, and pitch, and timbre, and volume. These are the properties of music, and music has the ability to find us and move us, and lift us up in ways that literal meanings can't."

~"War Crimes" (S3/E5)

"[My accurate oven thermometer] was presented to me as a gift from the personal sous chef to the King of... Fargo. Phil Baharnd. The man can sell a car like... well, like anything."

~"The Indians in the Lobby" (S3/E7)

"Look, I'm really not going to talk to you about my underwear."

~"H. Con - 172" (S3/E10)

"I was wrong! I was. I was just... I was wrong! Come on, you know that! Lots of times we don't know what right or wrong is, but lots of times we do and come on, this is one! I may not have had sinister intent at the outset, but there were plenty of opportunities for me to make it right. No one in government takes responsibility for anything anymore. We foster, we obfuscate, we rationalize. 'Everybody does it.' That's what we say. so we come to occupy a moral safe house where everyone's to blame so no one's guilty. I'm to blame. I was wrong!"

~"H. Con - 172" (S3/E10)

"I'm not messing around! This isn't barbecue night! I'm the Commander-in-Chief! Put your asses in the chairs!"

~"100,000 Airplanes" (S3/E11)

"I don't like the word *stress*. It's a Madison Avenue word. It's something that can be cured with flavored coffee and bath bubbles."

~"Night Five" (S3/E13)

"Whatever happened to Pong, huh? It was great, it was relaxing, it had that very satisfying sound?"

~"Enemies Foreign and Domestic" (S3/E16)

"If a guy is a good neighbor, if he puts in a day, if every once in a while he laughs, if every once in a while he thinks about somebody else and, above all else, if he can find his way to compassion and, and tolerance - then he's my brother, I don't give a damn if he didn't get past finger-painting. What I can't stomach are people who're out to convince people that the educated are soft and privileged, and out to make them feel like they're less than, you know, 'He may be educated, but I'm plain-spoken, just like you!' Especially when we know that education can be a silver bullet! It can be the silver bullet, Toby! For crime, poverty, unemployment, drugs, hate..."

~"Hartsfield's Landing" (S3/E14)

"Boo Boo, I gave up on getting you out the door in the late Seventies. Plus, it's your birthday. You're old, and you don't move around that fast."

~"Dead Irish Writers" (S3/E15)

"I think we might be talking about a .22 caliber mind in a .357 Magnum world."

~"The US Poet Laureate" (S3/E16)

"I'm not going to the bunker! There are going to be people who aren't going to the bunker, and when I get out, I'm not going to be able to tell them what to do anymore, and I like doing that. Let's get Abby to New Hampshire, but I'm not going to the bunker. And if you say I have to, I'm walking across the alley with the Chief Justice and I'm handing John Hoynes my resignation. And as soon as he's sworn in, I'm telling him to appoint me his Vice President because I'm not going to the bunker. If the agents come, the agents come, but tell Ron he'd better bring more than a couple of guys."

~"The Black Vera Wang" (S3/E19)

"In the future, if you're wondering, 'Crime - boy, I don't know' is when I decided to kick your ass!"

~"Posse Comitatus" (S3/E21)

"This is a time for American heroes, and we reach for the stars!"

~"20 Hours in America" (S4/E1)

"So what will I remember? What will I tell my grandchildren? I'll tell them that I stood on the Great Wall of China, and that I stood in the well of the US House of Representatives. I'll tell them that I sat with kings and cardinals and made an appointment to the Supreme Court, and I'll tell them that one morning in September I got to spend a few minutes with the men and women of Air Wing One. God bless you and your families and may he continue to shed his magnificent grace upon the United States of America!"

~"20 Hours in America" (S4/E1)

"300 IQ points between them - they can't find their way home. I swear to God, if Donna wasn't there, they'd have to buy a house."

~on Josh and Toby, "20 Hours in America" (S4/E1)

"More than any time in recent history, America's destiny is not of our own choosing. We did not seek, nor did we provoke an assault on our freedom and our way of life. We did not expect, nor did we invite a confrontation with evil. Yet the true measure of a people's strength is how they rise to master that moment when it does arrive. 44 people were killed a couple of hours ago at Kennison State University. Three swimmers from the men's team were killed and two others are in critical condition. When, after having heard the explosion from their practice facility, they ran into the fire to help get people out. Ran *into* the fire.

"The streets of heaven are too crowded with angels tonight. They're our students and our teachers and our parents and our friends. The streets of heaven are too crowded with angels, but every time we think we have measured our capacity to meet a challenge, we look up and we're reminded that that capacity may well be limitless. This is a time for American heroes! We will do what is hard; we will achieve what is great. This is a time for American heroes, and we reach for the stars! God bless their memory, God bless you, and God bless the United State of America! Thank you."

~"20 Hours in America" (S4/E1)

"Listen, I know we're here for a serious purpose, for a sober purpose, but I wanted to say I've never been a part of a street gang before, and that's basically what we are - a pretty well-financed one - but anyway, I wanted to say it feels good, and I think when we're done with this meeting, I think we should go out and get girls, and I don't know, maybe knock over a fruit stand or something."

~"College Kids" (S4/E2)

"'Let's stick some arsenic into President Bartlet's drinking water and see if he delegates responsibility to the World Bank then!' *President* Bartlet. You referred to me and to the office with respect. You're a class act!"

~"College'Kids" (S4/E2)

"There are times when we're 50 states, and there are times when we're one country, and have national needs. And the way I know this is that Florida didn't fight Germany in World War II, or establish civil rights. You think states should do the governing, wall-to-wall. That's a perfectly valid opinion. But your state of Florida got $12.6 billion in federal money last year - from Nebraskans, and Virginians, and New Yorkers, and Alaskans, with their Eskimo poetry. $12.6 out of a state budget of $50 billion. I'm supposed to be using this time for a question, so here it is: Can we have it back, please?"

~"Game On" (S4/E5)

"There are big signs! You can't park there! They *should* get towed! I hope they get towed to Queens and the Triboro is closed and there's a big craft show at Shea, a flea market or a tractor show!"

~"Arctic Radar" (S4/E9)

"'You must be the change' - is that it? 'You must be the change you wish to see in the world.' Sounds too much like Eastern philosophy."

~"Commencement" (S4/E21)

"There's a Korean word, *han*. I looked it up. There is no literal English translation; it's a state of mind; of soul, really. A sadness; a sadness so deep no tears will come. And yet still, there's hope."

~"Han" (S5/E4)

"All day we've been talking about my legacy, my portrait, what's going to be carved on my tombstone... Maybe we pay a little more attention to what's being rendered - and the rendering takes care of itself."

~"Slow News Day" (S5/E12)

"You were both participants of a top-secret exercise tonight, and for the time being it's going to have to remain top secret. If I'm ever looking this in the face, I hope I've got folks beside me like the two of you."

~to Charlie and Debbie, "Slow News Day" (S5/E20)

"...in 50, 60 years, some guy with a camcorder will track down some old codger who used to work here on the kitchen staff, and he'll tell the story of how I thought Stan Musial was a pediatrician in Abbey's medical school class."

~"Memorial Day" (S5/E22)

"I'm just saying, you drop me, that's a moment that follows you the rest of your life."

> ~to Curtis, who is carrying him, "Impact Winter" (S6/E9)

"My fellow Americans, in 1961, President John F. Kennedy bought some cigars. They happened to be from a country called Cuba. And since that day, nearly 45 years ago, no American has been able to do it again. And it's time for that to change.

"This is not about cigars, of course, but about our relationship with a country that is only 90 miles away. Change is not going to come easy. It won't be a change without passionate discussion and disagreement. But a change there can, and will, and must be.

"The Cuban people and the Cuban-American people have suffered too long under intolerable circumstances on both shores. My dream is that every one of the hundreds of thousands of Cubans who draw lottery cards every year to win one of the 20,000 slots allowing them to come to America in search of a better life and freedom will finally have the chance to find that freedom in their own country and that the one-and-a-half million Cuban-Americans who have for so many decades, longed to return to their homes will finally have the chance to once again see the land of their fathers and forefathers."

> ~"Ninety Miles Away" (S6/E19)

"I know you think this is probably old-fashioned, but, frankly, it's much more humane than it used to be. Abbey's father made me take a six-hour hike with him through the woods outside Mt. Pelier in the dead of winter. At least it felt like six hours. Of course I was still a grad student then, whereas you're almost a tenured professor. Isn't that right?"

> ~to Vic, his son-in-law-to-be, "The Wedding" (S7/E9)

"You're too young to remember Duck and Cover. We'd hide under our little wooden desks at school. At some point they stopped the drills. The threat was still there - they just stopped having the drills. I guess the realized a piece of plywood wasn't going to protect us against an atomic blast."

~to CJ, "Duck and Cover" (S7/E12)

Sorkinisms

Great writers steal from the best, and Aaron Sorkin is no exception: across four television series and more than twice that many movies, he was raided his own canon for material, over and over.

So common is Sorkin's self-stealing that the stolen bits have their own endearing name: *Sorkinisms*. True fans, who know now just *The West Wing* but the whole of the Sorkinverse, will have long since picked up on this.

There are dozens and dozens of them, and you can see the fan-assembled supercuts that place them side-by-side simply by searching "Sorkinisms" on YouTube.

Here are some of the best:

"Somebody's going to have to explain to me the

virtual of a proportional response!"

~President Andrew Shepherd, *The American President*
~President Jed Bartlet, *The West Wing*

"I'd already moved on to other things in my head."

~Sam Seaborn, *The West Wing*
~Matt Albie, *Studio 60 on the Sunset Strip*

"I hate his breathing guts!"

~Natalie Hurley, *Sports Night*
~Donna Moss, *The West Wing*: "...your..."
Harriet Hayes, *Studio 60 on the Sunset Strip*

*"Tell the press, don't tell the press –
it's entirely up to you."*

~President Andrew Shepherd to Sidney Ellen Wade,
    The American President: "Answer [the questions],
    don't answer them..."
~Abbey Bartlet to Dr. Lee, *The West Wing*

*"The only thing you had to do to make me happy was
come home at the end of the day."*

"The only thing you have to do to make me and your

mom happy is come home at the end of the day.”

~Jed Bartlet to Ellie, *The West Wing*
~Casey McCall to his son Charlie, *Sports Night*

“I’m not other people!”
“Don’t talk to me like I’m other people!”

~Natalie Hurley, *Sports Night*
~Dan Rydell, *Sports Night*
~Abbey Bartlet, *The West Wing*
~Network executive to Toby Ziegler, *The West Wing*

“Were you distracted by a bumblebee?”

~Toby Ziegler, *The West Wing*
~Mackenzie McHale, *The Newsroom*

“...like I got screwed with my pants on!”
“...talk about getting screwed with your pants on...”
“I’m gonna screw ‘em with their pants on!”

~Toby Ziegler, *The West Wing*
~Debbie Fiderer, *The West Wing*
~Josh Lyman, *The West Wing*

“More and more, we’ve come to expect less and less

from each other..."

~Dan Rydell, *Sports Night*
~Sen. Tony Marino, *The West Wing*
(Aaron Sorkin also used this line in a commencement address.)

"I think she's all about Eve..."

~Jed Bartlet, *The West Wing*
~Jordan McDeere, *Studio 60 on the Sunset Strip*

"I'm really quite something!"
"It was really quite something!"

~Josh Lyman, *The West Wing*
~Matt Albie, *Studio 60 on the Sunset Strip*
~Dana Whitaker, *Sports Night*

"I go home when you go home!"

~Marget Hooper to Leo McGarry, *The West Wing*
~Suzanne to Matt Albie, *Studio 60 on the Sunset Strip*

"If you haven't seen CJ do 'The Jackal', you haven't seen Shakespeare the way it's meant to be done!"

"If you haven't seen Davis Love play Pebble Beach, you haven't seen Shakespeare the way it was meant to

be played!"

~Sam Seaborn, *The West Wing*
~Casey McCall, *Sports Night*

"I have legs that go all the way down to the floor..."

~Amy Gardner, *The West Wing*
~Casey McCall, *Sports Night*: "Her legs go..."

"Eat 'em up!"

~Dana Whitaker, *Sports Night*
~ Leo McGarry, *The West Wing*
~ Josh Lyman, *The West Wing*
~Harriet Hayes, *Studio 60 on the Sunset Strip*

"Well, that was predictable..."

~Josh Lyman, *The West Wing*
~Tom Jeter, *Studio 60 on the Sunset Strip*

"Your garbage can's on fire."

~Natalie Hurley to Dana Whitaker, *Sports Night*
~Will Bailey to Toby Ziegler, *The West Wing*

"...for reasons passing understanding..."

~President Andrew Shepherd, *The American President*
~Toby Ziegler, *The West Wing*
~Jed Bartlet, *The West Wing*
~Matt Albie, *The West Wing*

~Will MacAvoy, *The Newsroom*

"I don't always know the right thing to do, Lord, but I

think the fact that I want to please you pleases you.”

~Isaac Jaffe, *Sports Night*
~Leo McGarry, *The West Wing*

“This isn't happening...”

~Sydney Ellen Wade, *The American President*
~Sam Seaborn, *The West Wing*
~Toby Ziegler, *The West Wing*
~CJ Cregg, *The West Wing*
~Simon Stiles, *Studio 60 on the Sunset Strip*

“Bring it, boss!”

~Casey McCall to Isaac Jaffe, *Sports Night*
~CJ Cregg to President Bartlet, *The West Wing*

“This will get worse before it gets better!”

~Sen. Andy Ritter, *The West Wing*
~NSA Nancy McNally, *The West Wing*

“...as if it matters how a man falls down!”

~Jeremy Goodwin, *Sports Night*
~Toby Ziegler, *The West Wing*
 from *The Lion in Winter*, Jed Bartlet's favorite movie

“It's almost hard to believe...”

~Dana Whitaker, *Sports Night*

~Dan Rydell, *Sports Night*
~Jed Bartlet, *The West Wing* (twice)
~CJ Cregg, *The West Wing* (twice)
~Josh Lyman, *The West Wing*
~Joey Lucas (through her interpreter Kenny), *The West Wing*
~Will McAvoy, *The Newsroom*

"That's the cost of doing business."

~Leo McGarry, *The West Wing*
~Jordan McDeere, *Studio 60 on the Sunset Strip*

"What do you want from me?"

~Natalie Hurley to Dana Whitaker, *Sports Night*
~Jed Bartlet to Leo McGarry, *The West Wing*
~Will Bailey to Elsie Snuffin, *The West Wing*
~Danny Tripp to Simon Stiles, *Studio 60 on the Sunset Strip*

"I'm not that guy!"

~Dan Rydell, *Sports Night*
~Jed Bartlet, *The West Wing*
~Simon Stiles, *Studio 60 on the Sunset Strip*

"Bet your ass!"

~Isaac Jaffe, *Sports Night*
~Margaret Hooper, *The West Wing*
~Leo McGarry, *The West Wing*
~Donna Moss, *The West Wing*
~Jack Rudolph, *Studio 60 on the Sunset Strip*

"Really?

"Yeah!"
"Really?
"Yeah!"

~Sam Seaborn and Toby Ziegler, *The West Wing*
~Lucy Kenwright and Tom Jeter, *Studio 60 on the Sunset Strip*

"Was that supposed to be funny?"

~President Jed Bartlet to God Almighty, *The West Wing*
~Ricky Tahoe to Danny Tripp, *Studio 60 on the Sunset Strip*

"My man has come back to me!"

~Natalie Hurley, *Sports Night*
~Donna Moss, *The West Wing*: "My man! You came back to me!"

"This isn't TV camp..."

~Sam Donovan, *Sports Night*
~Danny Tripp, *Studio 60 on the Sunset Strip*

"...it isn't important that everybody gets to play!"

~Toby Ziegler, *The West Wing*
~Danny Tripp, *Studio 60 on the Sunset Strip*

"I'm like Tippi Hedren around here!"

~Donna Moss, *The West Wing*
~Casey McCall, *Sports Night*: "...in there!"

"6 to 5 and pick 'em..."

~Rep. Doc Long, *Charlie Wilson's War*
~Leo McGarry, *The West Wing*
~Jim Harper, *The Newsroom*

"Just sign the damn thing!"

~Margaret Hooper to Leo McGarry, *The West Wing*
~Harriet Hayes to Matt Albie, *Studio 60 on the Sunset Strip*

"Eyes front, mister!"

~Jeremy Goodwin to Chris the studio tech, *Sports Night*
~President Bartlet to Sam Seaborn, *The West Wing*

"Can I help you?"

~Sam Seaborn, *The West Wing* (twice)
~Danny Tripp, *Studio 60 on the Sunset Strip*
~Matt Albie, *Studio 60 on the Sunset Strip*

"That's the cost of doing business!"

~Leo McGarry, *The West Wing*
~Jordan McDeere, *Studio 60 on the Sunset Strip*

...and, last but certainly not least,

"We don't have time to do things one at a time!"

~Lewis Rothschild, *The American President*
~Sam Seaborn, *The West Wing*

~TWW~

Legitimate Dude Sightings

Rob Lowe famously didn't stick it out through *The West Wing*'s seven seasons; he left the show toward the end of the fourth year. From there, he went right back into television with two series of his own: *The Lyon's Den*, a legal drama in which he starred, and *Dr. Vegas*, where he played a doctor. Neither series took off.

That didn't stop him; he's done a great deal more:

- He starred as Chris Traeger in 77 episodes of *Parks and Recreation*;
- He appeared in two episodes of *Salem's Lot*;
- He did six episodes of *Californication* as Eddie Nero;
- He appeared as himself on *Franklin & Bash*;
- He appeared twice as the randy alien Darulio on the *Star Trek* love letter *The Orville*;
- He's guest-hosted *Jimmy Kimmel Live!* twice;
- He was The Simpson's episode "The Very Hungry Caterpillars";
- He reunited with his Eighties Brat Pack alums in Andrew McCarthy's documentary about them, *Brats*, in 2024.

The Top 10 Leo Moments

Like his boss, Leo shines particularly bright in several key scenes. There are more (as they are with all the characters), but this is a start:

"You don't have to!"

With his gruff exterior and no-nonsense style, it's easy to overlook the fact that one of Leo's greatest strengths is encouraging those around him. He's a coach, but more – able to nudge those he cares about into reaching for their very best selves.

In "Let Bartlet Be Bartlet", he does this for his best friend, a president who is wrestling with having shied away from the challenges that drew him to the office in the first place. Leo makes the case that all he has to do is lead, and those loyal to him, "these people who would walk into fire if you told them to," will give him their very best.

"I don't want to feel like this anymore," Jed Bartlet says.

"You don't have to!" Leo assures him.

"That's your chief of staff!"

In one of the very best Leo moments, Leo himself doesn't say a word.

President Bartlet is about to deliver the State of the Union address, meaning a designated survivor – a Cabinet member in the line of succession – is left behind in the Oval Office.[9] As he's about to leave, Jed Bartlet gives him a checklist of things to do if the world goes to hell: "You got a best friend?" Yes! "Is he smarter than you?" Yes! "Would you trust him with your life?" Yes!

"That's your chief of staff."

...and Leo, unseen by the two, is shown in his own office nearby, overhearing those warm and loving words. It's a beautiful testimony,

---

[9] In "He Shall, from Time to Time..."

from the man who knows him best, of who he is.

"We had a responsibility to live our lives with integrity!"

Leo had maintained a life-long friendship with one of his military buddies – Kenny O'Neal, who (like Leo) became a successful executive after his service. When a powerful senator begins investigating O'Neal, now a military contractor, for corruption, Leo leaps to his friend's defense, determined to testify on his behalf (though Josh and the President aren't about to allow that).

His friend likewise refuses to let Leo take such a step, confessing that the corruption allegations are true. Leo is devastated.

"Men died for us!" Leo laments, in tears, in a private moment with Jed, as Crosby, Stills and Nash sing in the background. He is referring to the Vietnam War, when he and O'Neal were shot down in enemy territory, and O'Neal carried him to safety. "We had a responsibility to live our lives with integrity and honesty, to honor their sacrifice!"[10]

It's a powerful, intimate scene, one that unveils Leo's earnest commitment to living his life according to the highest moral standard.

"Everything else is crap!"

Ainsley Hayes is a Republican. She is a feisty, outspoken, brilliant Republican, and when she kicks Sam's ass on *Capital Beat* (much to Josh and Toby's amusement), President Bartlet instructs Leo to hire her for the White House counsel's office. Leo pushes back – why in the world would we do that? Well, because the President likes smart people who disagree with him ("In This White House").

Once he realizes the President is serious, he commits to getting it done, and he brings Ainsley in. She herself has doubts: she is no fan of the Bartlet Administration, and doesn't believe she'll be accepted.

Leo once again becomes the great encourager, offering her warm and supportive reassurance:

"He wants to hear from you," he tells her with a comforting smile.

---

[10] In "An Khe".

"The President's asking you to serve! And everything else is crap!"

"Let that be our legacy!"

Having encouraged President Bartlet to get off the bench and onto the field, Leo proceeds to give the senior staff notice that it's all about to get real (in "Let Bartlet Be Bartlet"). He gathers them in his office and puts them on notice:

"We're gonna lose some of these battles, and we might even lose the White House – but we're not gonna be threatened by issues! We're gonna put them front and center! We're gonna raise the level of public debate in this country – and let that be our legacy!"

"I've been walking around in a kind of daze for two weeks..."

Sitting before a Congressional committee, lights all over him and cameras soaking up his every word, Leo answers questions about his connection to and conversations with the President, concerning his MS. In flashback, we're taken back to a moment the two shared in the New Hampshire Governor's office four years earlier – and we're reminded that everything we've seen on *The West Wing*, every story we've heard, owes to Leo's inspiration to urge Jed Bartlet to run for president in the first place. He's the one who believed in his friend; he's the one who had the vision to see that Jed Bartlet could ascend to the nation's highest office, and make a real difference:[11]

"I've been walking around in a kind of daze for two weeks," he tells Jed, "and everywhere I go – planes, trains, restaurants, meetings – I find myself scribbling something down..." He pulls a napkin from his

---

[11] In "Bartlet for America".

pocket.

On the napkin is written, *Bartlet for America...*

"There's a reason he's a friend of ours!"

Leo doesn't just stand up for the staff and his old friends. He'll go to bat for anyone he believes worthy of defending.

When tech executive Jake Kimball's computer manufacturing company, Antares, is forced to recall tens of millions of computers over a chip defect, Leo immediately urges the President to have Congress guarantee a loan to bail them out, so the company doesn't go under.[12] The free-market economist President doesn't want to get involved, because in his eyes, what's happening to Kimball and his company is just too bad – it's how markets work.

Leo won't accept that: "You said it was carelessness, and I don't believe carelessness has to exist for a mistake to be made!"

So passionate is Leo in his defense of Kimball, pointing out that he is a man of ethics and honesty comparable to themselves, that President Bartlet comes through with a solution that will support the survival of Antares. He and Leo manage to take a stand for the values they share with Kimball without resorting to political favoritism.

"I think the world owes it to itself..."

Leo is a strong supporter of the NMD system, a space-based ballistic missile countermeasure that is expensive and fraught with technical complexities and challenge. President Bartlet (and many others) considers it a boondoggle ("that preposterous contraption," in Mrs. Landingham's words), and Lord John Marbury thinks it is both ill-conceived and illegal (in "The Drop-In").

But Leo's belief in the project is rooted, not in military rationalization or even political gamesmanship, but in the honest conviction that it is a step in the direction humanity needs to go – and he makes that argument to Marbury, displaying the earnest

---

[12] In "Enemies Foreign and Domestic".

motivations that ultimately define him as a public servant:

"I think the world invented a nuclear weapon," he says. "I think the world owes it to itself to see if it can't invent something that would make it irrelevant."

"You and I will give each other a second chance..."

When a leak about one of the Vice President's staffers gets Sam's attention, he connects the leak to the private information about Leo's treatment for addiction that made its way into the hands of Congressman Lillienfield. He traces the leak to a White House staffer, Karen Larsen, and promptly fires her (in "Take Out the Trash Day").

Leo summons her as she is about to leave the building. The two of them speak, and he learns that the reason she did it was that she had learned of Leo's issues with alcoholism and addiction, reminding her of own father's alcoholism. Leo feels a strong sense of empathy, as the pain and exhaustion of the consequences of alcoholism are written all over the young woman's face. He proceeds to join her in vulnerability, relating a small bit of his own struggle. He makes a decision, one that radiates his humanity and compassion.

"Did you like working at the White House?"

She nods.

"Then why don't you go unpack your carton, and you and I will give each other a second chance?"

"This guy falls into a hole..."

In the aftermath of the Rosslyn shooting, Josh – who was almost killed – is showing severe symptoms of PTSD. Leo calls in a psychiatrist to help Josh cope with the trauma (in "Noël").

The session is long and difficult, but Josh is able to get to the bottom of what's been triggering him – not a cure, but a first step onto the road of recovery.

As he's leaving the White House that evening, he finds Leo waiting for him in the lobby. This supportive gesture, in keeping with his arranging the session in the first place, is a testament to Leo's role in Josh's life – not just as concerned boss, but as compassionate friend.

Josh is moved by the gesture of support, and reciprocates in the following year (in "Bartlet for America").

The story Leo tells Josh to explain their connection – "This guy falls into a hole" – acknowledges that while their respective struggles might have different roots, the solution is the same: standing by one another.

"I've been down here before, and I know the way out!"

The Best of Leo McGarry

"Because I'm tired of it, year after year after year after year! Having to choose between the lesser of who cares? Of trying to get myself excited about a candidate who can speak in complete sentences! Of setting the bar so low, I can hardly look at it. They say a good man can't get elected President. I don't believe that, do you?
~"In the Shadow of Two Gunmen, Pt. I" (S2/E1)

"The President likes smart people who disagree with him. He wants to hear from you. The President's asking you to serve – and everything else is crap!"
~"In This White House" (S2/E4)

"This guy's walking down a street, when he falls in a hole. The walls are so steep, he can't get out. A doctor passes by, and the guy shouts up, 'Hey you! Can you help me out?' The doctor writes him a prescription, throws it down the hole and moves on. Then a priest comes along, and the guy shouts up 'Father, I'm down in this hole, can you help me out?' The priest writes out a prayer, throws it down in the hole and moves on. Then a friend walks by. 'Hey Joe, it's me, can you help me out?' And the friend jumps in the hole! Our guy says 'Are you stupid? Now we're both down here!' and the friend says, 'Yeah, but I've been down here before, and I know the way out.'"
~"Noël" (S2/E10)

"Yeah, that's 'cause I made fun of her shoes and Sam said there were nuclear weapons in Kyrgyzstan and Donna went to clear up the mix-up and accidentally left her underwear."

~"The Leadership Breakfast" (S2/E11)

"All right, shut the hell up, everybody! I've fired more people than you before breakfast!"

~"Somebody's Going to Emergency, Somebody's Going to Jail" (S2/E16)

"We're not gonna stop, soften, detour, postpone, circumvent, obfuscate, or trade a single one of our goals to allow for whatever extracurricular nonsense is coming our way in the next few days, weeks, and months!"

~"18th and Potomac" (s2/E21)

"I take a bullet for the President! He doesn't take one for me!"

~"H. Con - 172" (s3/E10)

"What a waste, since the moon! My generation never got the future it was promised! 35 years later, cars, air travel's the same. We don't even have the Concorde anymore. Technology stopped. [The personal computer], a more efficient delivery system for gossip and pornography. Where's my jet pack, my colonies on the Moon? Just a waste!"

~"The Warfare of Genghis Khan" (s5/E13)

"You campaign in poetry, you govern in prose."

~"Talking Points" (s5/E19)

"With Nancy McNally out of the country, you're going to have to be our go-to... I was gonna say 'guy'. The problem with English: 'guy' is wrong, 'gal' is patronizing, and 'person' sounds arch."

~"Gaza" (s5/E21)

"I lived through the first Cold War. One was enough."

~"A Change is Gonna Come" (s6/7)E

"But once in a while, on certain days, when they take down the flag out that window at sunset - you know you did something. And that ain't all bad!"

~"A Change is Gonna Come" (s6/E7)

"There are no stupid ideas. Actually there are, I don't know why people say that."

~"Impact Winter" (s6/E9)

"The both of us, sir, this is our last game. Let's leave it all out on the field."

~"365 Days" (s6/E12)

~TWW~

The Supreme Court comes up repeatedly in *The West Wing*. Here are the real-world justices who are mentioned...

<u>Chief Justices</u>
Warren Burger in "The Short List"
Charles Evans Hughes, in "20 Hours in LA"
John Marshall, in "Separation of Powers"
Earl Warren, in "Eppur Si Muove"

<u>Associate Justices</u>
Louis Brandeis, in "Bad Moon Rising"
Oliver Wendall Holmes, in "On the Day Before"
William O. Douglas, in "Separation of Powers"
John Marshall Harlan, in "The Supremes"
Robert H. Jackson, in "Welcome to Wherever You Are"

The Missing Justices

The *West Wing*'s Supreme Court emerges early on, in the first half of the first season, as President Bartlet is tasked with replacing the retiring Justice Joseph Crouch – his first Supreme Court appointment ("The Short List").

That marvelous episode has Bartlet reneging on the safe choice of Peyton Cabot Harrison III, when Sam discovers that he does not believe in Constitutional protection of privacy, and going with the riskier but far more progressive choice of the brilliant, decisive Roberto Mendoza – a Latino.

So – Crouch is out, Mendoza is in, and as we move forward in the series, we learn of two other serving justices – Ronald Driefort and Chief Justice Roy Ashland.

We learn about Driefort in "And It's Surely to Their Credit", when the temperamental White House Counsel Lionel Tribbey bursts into Leo's office to throw a fit, and meets Ainsley Hayes – who is reporting for her first day of work. Turns out she clerked for Driefort, which does not impress Tribbey, as Driefort is "intolerant towards gays, lesbians, blacks, unions, women, poor people, and the 1st, 4th, 5th and 9th amendments!"

We had seen the seated Supreme Court at the beginning of "Take This Sabbath Day". There are, correctly, eight justices - Crouch would have been absent, and the not-yet-confirmed Mendoza would have yet been seated. We'll come back to them.

In later seasons, we learn the name of the Chief Justice – Roy Ashland, who is 82 years old and starting to lose it – who has been chief 12 years as of the sixth year of the Bartlet Administration. That would have been seven years at the time of Mendoza's appointment (first mentioned in "Inauguration, Pt. I" and first seen in "Separation of Powers").

But Roy Ashland isn't among the justices seen in "Take This Sabbath Day".

The reason, of course, is because the character hadn't been invented yet in *TWW*'s first season. We can understand that, and let it slide; but the Supreme Court sloppiness, sadly, grows worse.

Associate Justice Owen Brady dies unexpectedly at the end of "Eppur Si Muove", meaning the President has another seat to fill. Yet he says, "Filling another seat on the court may be the only lasting thing I do in this office," as though he hadn't done it already, a point he makes while chastising the Lord God Almighty in "Two Cathedrals".

Now, we're back to eight justices again, and Owen Brady was necessarily one of the justices we saw sitting on the bench in the opening of "Take This Sabbath Day" (as was Ronald Driefort).

Josh has the inspiration to get two justices for one, following Brady's death – bring in the very liberal Evelyn Baker Lang to replace the very liberal Roy Ashland, and get her past the Judiciary Committee pit bulls by letting the committee appoint the conservative of their choice to Brady's seat ("The Supremes").

So we now have Lang and Christopher Mulready, the committee's choice, on the court – and Driefort is necessarily still there. That's three.

Mulready speaks the names of the others – Carmine, Lafayette, Hoyt, Clark, and Brannaghan – and that brings us to eight.

The ninth is Sharon Day, summoned to the Oval Office to swear in Glen Allen Walken as President in "Twenty Five". The immediate objection is that President Bartlet just told Charlie to bring in a federal judge, and that's all she was – but no, when she arrives, Charlie introduces her as "Madam Justice Sharon Day". Federal judges are not called 'Justice'.[13]

Roberto Mendoza, President Bartlet's first appointment, is never mentioned in the episode. It's a toss-up whether Mendoza or Day is the ninth justice.

We could argue that Mulready omitted any mention of Mendoza in his Oval Office chat with the President because they were talking about moderates, in the mold of appointee-wannabe Brad Shelton, making the point that Carmine, Lafayette, Hoyt, Clarke, and Brannigan were all moderates. Mendoza was anything but moderate. (This would also be the reason Mulready didn't mention Driefort in his list: he, too, was anything but moderate.)

---

[13] Just to be difficult, we'll point out that Sharon Day is not the female justice we saw on the bench in "Take This Sabbath Day".

And this creates a serious problem: the episode frames Ashland as the court's only liberal voice, when Josh says to Toby, "We've got centrists. We've got six of them. Plus two staunch conservatives [Brady and Driefort] plus Justice Ashland." (Josh is counting Brady here as if he were still alive, which he isn't, but his point remains.)

And any argument that Mendoza became a centrist once he ascended to the bench collapses immediately: if he had, it supports the contention that Ashland was the lone liberal - but then Mulready would have been compelled to list him with the other moderates.

Mendoza, then, was certainly still on the court, and certainly still a liberal?

By objective count, the final tally is two staunch liberals, two staunch conservatives, and five centrists. The moderates just *barely* out-number the non-moderates.

Our conclusion: Josh Lyman can't count!

~TWW~

Legitimate Dude Sightings

Alllison Janney was singled out for the role of CJ by Aaron Sorkin largely on the strength of her pratfall comic turn in *Primary Colors*, but since being CJ, she's lit up big screens and small screens alike:

- Roles in *Juno*, *The Help*, *Finding Dory*, *The Girl on the Train*, and more than a dozen other films;
- A star turn in *Lou* (2022), a crime thriller produced by JJ Abrams;
- On TV, she guest-starred as herself on *Studio 60 on the Sunset Strip*;
- Guest spots on *Two and a Half Men*, *Family Guy*, *Lost*, *The Simpsons*, *Veep*, *Key & Peele*, and many others;
- She appeared as herself on Michael Douglas's *The Kominsky Method*;
- She had the title role on the sitcom *Mom* for 8 years, logging 170 episodes – more than *TWW!* – as Bonnie Plunkett.

Inconsistencies!

The show's handling of its Supreme Court is by no means the only inconsistency. There are many! It might seem odd to poke at them, but – as with *Star Trek* – pondering those inconsistencies and trying to reconcile them is nerdy, nerdy fun, is invigorating mental exercise, and pulls us deeper into TWW's exquisite alternate reality.

Here we go!

Leo's Sobriety

One of the most glaring continuity errors in WestWingWorld is Leo McGarry's sobriety. It's established early on, in "Take Out the Trash Day", when information about his treatment for alcoholism and drug addiction is leaked. Confronting the leaker, a young White House staffer who thought she was doing the right thing based on her experience with her own alcoholic father, he kicks off a timeline for his sobriety in a comment he makes to her:

"I'm not cured. You don't get cured. I haven't had a drink or a pill in six and a half years, which isn't to say I won't have one tomorrow."

He says this in 1999 (*West Wing* time), the second year of the Bartlet Administration. Depending on the time of year, that puts his Sierra-Tucson treatment in 1993.

Yet we have two conflicting data points: the first emerges in "Bartlet for America", when he recalls the final days of the first campaign. At time of the final presidential debate, he falls off the wagon and has a drink with some potential donors, following it up with a binge, which one of the donors learns of (and later tries to bring up to humiliate him).

The second is in flashback to 1995, when he was in Cuba, participating as Secretary of Labor in quiet conversations with veterans of the Bay of Pigs in hopes of establishing a dialog between Cubans and Cuban-Americans that might change the relationship between the US and Cuba.[14] Kate Harper, then with the CIA, came across him there,

---

14 In "Ninety Miles Away".

drunk out of his mind – just two years before Bartlet for America, and just three years before becoming Chief of Staff.

Texas in the First Election

Did President Bartlet win Texas in the first election or didn't he?

This one is so muddled that there's no way to call it one way and just say there's some inconsistency; the show says outright that Barlet won Texas, and that Bartlet *didn't* win Texas.

That they lost Texas is stated in right up front, in the second episode of the show – "Post Hoc, Ergo Propter Hoc". In an Oval Office discussion of how the President looks in funny hats, CJ says, very plainly, "We got whomped in Texas!" – and Josh agrees.

Not long after, Vice President John Hoynes asks, in an argument with the President, "What did I ever do to you, except deliver the South?"[15] Now – this, of course, is an ambiguous point, because he says "the South", not specifying Texas; but he's from Texas, he was a Texas senator. Do we suppose that he delivered all of the South *except* his home state?

But then Josh says, in a conversation about the upcoming re-election campaign, "If we lose Texas this time..." – implying that they won Texas in the first election!

Hoynes and Ethanol

While we're on the subject of Hoyes, there's a lot of mystery about his position on ethanol.

In "20 Hours in LA", there's an ethanol tax credit vote coming up in the Senate, and the anticipated vote is 50-50 – meaning the Vice President will have to step in and break the tie. The Bartlet Administration wants it to pass; but Hoynes is solidly on record opposing ethanol, for reasons President Bartlet secretly agrees with. In the end, he's let off the hook, and doesn't have to flip-flop on his ethanol position.

But in "In the Shadow of Two Gunmen, Pt. I", as then-Senator

---

[15] In "Enemies".

Hoynes is leaving a staff meeting to speak privately with Josh, he tells the staff, "The rest of you should stay here and work on the ethanol tax credit."

And as the second Bartlet term is ending, and Hoynes is in the race to succeed him, ethanol is a big deal in Iowa, one of the first campaign stops (in "King Corn"). Descending on it for the caucus, the candidates – among which Hoynes was still counted, at the time – all have to address the Iowa Corn Growers Expo and state their position on ethanol, which Iowa corn growers produce. The other candidates – Bob Russell, Matt Santos, and Arnold Vinick – are all shown doing so, with Russell and Santos taking the ethanol pledge and Vinick taking the more honest stance of opposition to ethanol as a dead end, which is how Hoynes feels as well.

Hoynes addressing the corn growers isn't shown, though it absolutely must have happened. But we know he did the same thing Vinick did eight years earlier in the Bartlet for America campaign, because President Bartlet said so in "20 Hours in LA": "I want to tell you, a couple of years ago in Iowa, I really admired the way you hung in there on the ethanol tax credit. You went out to Iowa and said the same things you'd been saying in the Senate for eight years, even though you knew it wasn't going to play."

Hoynes isn't shown in the episode, but his position is discussed.

"We're sure Hoynes will flip?" a Russell staffer asks.

"Believe me, Hoynes is taking the pledge," Will Bailey answers. "This guy, if speaking to cannibals, will promise them missionaries."

Well... no, Will. We already know that Hoynes stood firm on his position the last time he'd addressed the Iowa Corn Growers, when even Jed Bartlet didn't.

And yet – if Hoynes *had* stood firm the second time around, why is nothing at all said about it? Everyone is abuzz because Arnold Vinick told it straight; is it conceivable that if one of the Democratic candidates had the same, it *wouldn't* have been the story of the week?

Bartlet's First Veto

This one's short and sweet:

Mark Gottfriend, host of *Capital Beat*, mediates a debate between Sam and Ainsley Hayes ("In This White House") about the President's

$1.5 billion education bill. He asks Sam, "Why is this bill better that its Republican counterpart that the President vetoed last year?"

President Bartlet's first veto, then, took place in the first year of his first term.

But...

In "Ways and Means", as the senior staff are discussing how to deal with a looming vote on an estate tax bill, political consultant Doug Wegland advises that if Congress passes it, the President should "take out the A-bomb; I think he's got to do something he's never done even once before... I think he's got to veto!"

We can't write this off as a mistake by an outsider (though Wegland, as a member of Bruno Gianelli's team, is not the kind of guy who could make such a mistake); CJ herself tells her press gaggle, soon after that, that the veto – which President Bartlet does – "...was his first veto since taking the office 33 months ago."

The President's Secret Service Codename

This one's even shorter/sweeter:

President Bartlet's Secret Service codename is established as "Eagle" in "Post Hoc, Ergo Propter Hoc".

But then it's changed to "Liberty" in "He Shall, From Time to Time..."[16]

Now, that's not so over-the-top; we learn in "In Excelsis Deo" that the Secret Service changes the codenames from time to time.

Except...

The President's codename is *back to Eagle* in "In the Shadow of Two Gunmen"! Even granting that the codenames change regularly, like laptop passwords in the workplace, going back to an old codename

---

[16] This codename is a nod to *The American President*, where it is used as President Andrew Shepherd's codename. The very first line of the movie is, in fact, "Liberty is moving."

entirely defeats the purpose of changing it in the first place!

The Many Attorneys General

This one is all over the place.

The first mention of the Bartlet Administration's Attorney General is made in "A Proportional Response" – not by name, but Leo states that he is black.

Except... he isn't. He's Dan Larson, and he's white as can be, when we meet him in "Lies, Damn Lies and Statistics".

His second-term successor, Alan Fisk (seen in "Abu el Banat") is likewise lily-white.

And we note that President's original nominee for the post, before his presidency began – Cornell Rooker – was black: "...the first African-American I've ever heard make sense of racial profiling," according to a right-wing Evangelical reporter speaking with CJ.

So... if all of the above are true, then the Bartlet Cabinet...

- started off by nominating a black racial profiler for AG, only to
- withdraw the nomination because of the racial profiling, then
- appointed an unnamed black AG, who only lasted a year,
- replaced by Dan Larson, who was followed in the next term by
- Alan Fisk.

Or... this is just a big inconsistency!

~TWW~

In "Mr. Willis of Ohio", there is a House roll call – alphabetical, as all such roll calls are. In the names called after Mr. Willis votes, Toby's ex – Congresswoman Wyatt – should be included. But she isn't.

The Top 12 Josh Moments

Like his boss, Leo shines particularly bright in several key scenes. There are more (as they are with all the characters), but this is a start:

"It's got a molted calf cover and original draft boards..."

As Toby quietly arranges the funeral of veteran indigent Walter Hufnagel,[17] Josh is mangling the word *mottled* (a joke that goes over the heads of most viewers) as he explains the Christmas gift he's given Donna – a first edition of *Heimlich Beckengruber on the Art and Artistry of Alpine Skiing*.

The theme is spot-on, but it's not quite what she was shooting for ("Skis would have killed you?"), but he made it special by writing a note inside. Reading the note, she fights back tears – and hugs him fiercely. He hugs her back.

And moments later, he peeks out of his office door, watching her re-read the note with a huge smile on her face.

Only they know what he wrote, but whatever it was, it was their first intimate connection – foreshadowing the much greater intimate connection to follow.

"YOU WANT A PIECE OF ME???"

Josh wins big. And he loses big (see "Josh Lyman's Greatest Hits", below). When his belligerent brinkmanship of Democratic Senator Chris Carrick goes too far, resulting in Carrick's defection from the Democratic Party, he is on the outs not only with the President and Leo, but the entire Democratic Party.

Those right next to him – Donna, and his intern Ryan Pierce – do what they can to help him save face. But his failure roils inside him, reminding him that surrender to his less noble impulses is a betrayal of his commitment to service. He's a fighter, and he sees enemies and

---

17 In "In Excelsis Deo".

agendas everywhere, but his biggest battle is within.

He can't, however, express it that cleanly. Riding in a cab with Ryan after dinner, he passes the Capitol Building and leaps from the car, shouting at it:

"HEY!!! You want a piece of me? I'm right here! I'm standing right here! Come on! Come on!"[18]

He is almost in tears. That this outburst happens right in front of Ryan is telling, as Ryan is the last person in front of whom he'd want to be vulnerable. His anguish is deep, his sense of failure overwhelming, and we can't help but sympathize: his mistakes have compromised him, and the depth of his regret speaks to the sincerity of his desire to serve, and serve well.

"What do you want, Mr. President?"

Josh has had a really hard time in the early months of the second Bartlet term. He really blew it with Senator Carrick, losing the Democrats an ally in a tough season. He's so in the doghouse that Leo has brought in his former colleague Angela Blake to handle some of Josh's portfolio.

But – as he always does – Josh bounces back. In the midst of a federal government shutdown and very public tussle with Speaker Haffley, President Bartlet listens to his team as they bandy desperate measures and painful compromises to bring the budget crisis to an end in the Roosevelt Room.[19] The President is openly grasping at straws. And Josh says the thing he needs to hear:

"What do *you* want, Mr. President?"

President Bartlet is galvanized by that question. He rises from the conference table and, against the advice of most of his advisors, announces that he is going to the Hill, hat in hand, to negotiate Haffley on his own turf – an act of unprecedented humility and conciliatory compromise.

And then, as the President shakes hand near his motorcade, Josh

---

[18] In "Disaster Relief".

[19] In "Shutdown".

does it again:

"Care to stretch your legs?"

Josh's suggestion that the presidential entourage walk, rather than drive, to the Capitol puts the Secret Service in a tizzy, but with a thousand cameras right there surrounding them, it's the best public relations move in the history of the American presidency: the nation sees, in real time, the President extending a humble and cooperative hand to a recalcitrant Congress.

Then Josh does it *again*, when the President is left sitting on a bench outside Haffley's office for all the cameras to see, as Haffley and the Majority Leader, caught off guard, stall to strategize:

"Let's go. *Right now.*"

Haffley and Royce emerge from their cave to an empty foyer, as the cameras follow the President and his party back to the White House. It is a moment of sweet victory for the embattled President, as the nation's sympathies swing his way. And Josh's redemption is complete.

> *"I am comforted in my certainty that he is doing his best to reach for all of it, and not just the McNuggets!"*

Faced with a serious re-elect challenge in Gov. Rob Ritchie, the staff has been learning all they can about the Republican governor of Florida. Turns out he's a disciple of a shallow self-help guru, so Josh ruins yet another of Donna's weekends by sending him to one of the guru's seminars. She returns to the office, feeling like she needs a shower (in "The Red Mass").

The guru is an empty sloganeer, explaining why Ritchie is, too. And one of his books, which Donna picked up, is loaded with out-of-context quotes by great thinkers. Donna questions the relevance of it all, and Josh offers a marvelous summation of why it's important to give deep consideration to the writings of the wise – that the problems a president must confront require more than mere slogans and memes. In the process, he passively reveals that he himself is that kind of serious person, summing his point with a question that honors the investment they've all made in Jed Bartlet:

"Is it possible we would be willing to require any less of the person sitting in that chair?"

"Yeah, Danny. We have a secret plan to fight inflation."

Josh is smart, capable, and shrewd, but he's also arrogant, smug, and condescending. When CJ is sidelined from her own briefing by a woot canow, Josh steps in to face the press – and bungles it, not bothering to mask his derision and contempt. He doesn't take the press seriously, and he has no problem making that perfectly clear.

But they take themselves seriously, and when Danny Concannon corners him on a point about the drop in unemployment, about which the Bartlet Administration has crowed, and the resulting impact on wages, Josh finds himself floundering. It's not enough that he botches his answer; he digs the hole deeper and deeper, grasping for lame humor to extricate himself, flaming out.

It's a classic crash-and-burn that very publicly throws his less admirable traits into high relief, but it's also a teaching moment. And in the end, his better angels return: when he good-naturedly tells the story at a college lecture series later that same week, we see that he can not only acknowledge his mistakes, but laugh at himself as he learns from them.

"I never learned what you do
after you think you like somebody..."

Josh is gifted in the art of politics, but addled in the art of love. Smitten by Amy Gardner, a fiery and capable activist and old college friend, he engages in lame and sophomoric hijinks in order to spend more time around her. She is smarter than he is, so it takes her no time at all to realize what's happening, and cuts to the chase by ambushing him on his own front steps.

And his response is redeeming: without blinking, he shifts into honest self-disclosure mode, soberly assuring her that the seriousness of his position precludes any dissembling about his intent. He goes much further than that – further than most men would! – and confesses right to her face that he comes by his ignorance of how to express himself honestly, as a product of insecurity.

She responds by kissing him.

It's a marvelous moment, one in which both we and Amy learn a great deal about Josh.

"You've got a pretty bad poker face..."

It's the beginning of the Bartlet for America campaign, before the first term, seen in "In the Shadow of Two Gunmen, Pt. I". Josh is off to see Gov. Jed Bartlet speak in Nashua, New Hampshire, not because he particularly wants to but because Leo McGarry asked him to – and Leo's an old friend of his dad.

On the way, he swings through New York City, dropping in on his old friend Sam Seaborn, an attorney with Gage Whitney. His trip may be a fool's errand, but he'd hedging his bets – he takes a swing at recruiting Sam for the Hoynes campaign. Even so, he acknowledges the possibility that Bartlet might be the right guy.

"If I see the real thing in Nashua – should I tell you about it?"

"You won't have to; you've got a pretty bad poker face!"

Jed Bartlet is the real thing, winning Josh over in a town hall meeting, and he swings back through New York ("In the Shadow of Two Gunmen, Pt. II") – standing outside the conference room at Sam's office, not saying a word, openly beaming. Terrible poker face!

Sam gets up and walks out on the meeting, his job, and his profession.

That moment says so much about both of them. We see the depth of their friendship, their trust in each other, their shared commitment to the ideals that Josh sees in Jed Bartlet – all of it, in a single moment.

"Go ahead..."

The Bartlet for America campaign is up and running, and as they prepare to pick up and move from Nashua to Charleston, Josh finds a young woman in his office, answering his phone.

"I'm Donna Moss, I'm your new assistant!"

Donna literally walked in off the street, crashing the campaign for no reason other than her desire to be part of it all. She and Josh do a walk-and-talk through the campaign office as she explains her careening background and vague qualifications. He is amused but unmoved, until they return to his office and he puts his foot down.

"I can't carry you, Donna! I got a lot of guys out there not making the trip."

"I'll pay my own way! I'll sleep on the floor, I'll sell my car. Eventually, you're going to put me on salary.

"I think I might be good at this. I think you might find me valuable."

The phone rings. He nods toward it as he hands her a campaign staff badge.

"Go ahead..."

Following his instincts, giving Donna a chance without any solid justification, makes for a beautiful moment – but it also speaks to his awareness of others. He saw in Donna, in a few short minutes, a flash of the dedication and commitment he nurtures within himself and delights in seeing in others.

> *"Governor, if you don't lose this election, it isn't going to be because you didn't try hard enough!"*

On the night of the Illinois primary, during the Bartlet for America campaign, Jed Bartlet takes the win – and Josh's father dies (in "In the Shadow of Two Gunmen, Pt. II").

At the airport, waiting for a flight to Connecticut, Josh is surprised at the approach of Gov. Bartlet, now flanked by Secret Service. Bartlet sits with him in the concourse, and they have their first real conversation.

It's a profound moment for them both: by his own admission, Bartlet has been "a real jackass" to Josh and the rest of the senior-staff-to-be, and he reaches out to Josh with authentic empathy and comfort in the face of his loss. Josh, who has a pathological tendency to shoulder guilt that isn't really his to shoulder, manages to open up to Bartlet, accepting the gesture with grace and wistful appreciation. It is the first real sign since he saw Bartlet speak in Nashua months earlier that he truly is the man Josh originally took him to be.

And this moment of emotional openness, prompted by Josh's graciousness, is what Jed Bartlet really needs, at the moment he really needs it: he tells Leo, as Josh heads for the gate – "Leo... I'm ready."

"You need to listen to me!!!"

Not long after being shot and almost killed in Rosslyn, Josh has a moment in the Oval Office with the President, Leo and Sam in which he disagrees with them about the political consequences of tapping into the Strategic Petroleum Reserve. They are dismissive of his concerns, as he is dismissive of their desire to move on.

And Josh Lyman flies off the handle at the President, there in the Oval Office, as Leo and Sam look on:

"You need to listen to me! You have to listen to me! I can't help you unless you listen to me!"

It is a shocking, unprecedented moment, breathtaking in its suddenness and intensity. Leo immediately realizes it's PTSD, the aftereffects of Josh's ordeal, and arranges for a specialist to see him.[20]

That scene, brilliantly performed, is a powerful look into the ravages of PTSD – and an impactful revelation of just how deep Josh's need to serve and make a difference, how much he needs to be taken seriously as part of the process.

"...his music just left the solar system!"

After treating a group of visiting NASA officials and scientists dismissively, Josh rethinks his attitude when one of the group – a particularly brainy and attractive one – persistently urges him to take a look at what it is he's dismissing. They do an evening run out of the city with a powerful telescope, and she gives him a tour of the skies.[21]

Donna pokes at him over it, suggesting that his change of heart was

---

[20] In "Noël".

[21] In "The Warfare of Genghis Khan".

all about the NASA scientist's batting eyes, but something else is going on: he digs into the subject in earnest, giving thought to the inspirational value of a renewed NASA mission to get to Mars.

Sharing his findings with Donna, he notes the timeliness of the *Voyager* probe's crossover into interstellar space. He tells her that *Voyager* is carrying greetings, messages, pictures, and music from Earth, in case any deep-space neighbors ever find it. Josh is swept up in the perspective-expanding romance of it all, which is stoking his own sense of inspiration. He manages to bring Donna along when he lists the music Voyager is including – Gregorian chants, Chuck Berry, and...

"'Dark Was The Night, Cold Was The Ground' by '20s bluesman Blind Willie Johnson, whose stepmother blinded him when he was seven by throwing lye in is his eyes after his father had beaten her for being with another man. He died, penniless, of pneumonia after sleeping bundled in wet newspapers in the ruins of his house that burned down.

"But his music just left the solar system."

"The going-with-you part was all me..."

The will-they-or-won't-they tension between Josh and Donna was a high-wire act for all seven years, all the more tenuous after her resignation and defection to Will Bailey and the Russell campaign. But the subsequent final stretch of the Santos contest for the presidency, once again reunited, clearly refocused Josh on that tension – and, probably, how it must have felt in the early days.

The will-they-or-won't-they is finally settled, and she lets him know that they can't just leave it open-ended; they will both be working in the White House. At some point, they will have to make the decision whether or not to commit to what they've started.

As all this is happening, Josh is well and truly fried from a grueling year on the road, and Sam dresses him down with an ultimatum: Josh needs to get on a plane and take some time off – or Sam will get on a plane and never come back (in "Transition").

Josh isn't about to lose Sam, so he capitulates, letting Santos know he'll be away for a while and Sam will handle things.

Josh gets on a plane – and Donna sits down next to him. And we finally see what we've waited years to see – a decisive, willing-to-commit Josh Lyman, making the right decision for the right reasons.

"May I say, a truly excellent notion?" Donna says.

"Sam's," he explains. Credit where it's due.

She smiles. "Of course!"

"The vacation," he clarifies. "The going-with-you part was all me..."

The Best of Josh Lyman

"Victory is mine, victory is mine! Great day in the morning, people, Victory is mine!"

~"Post Hoc, Ergo Propter Hoc" (s1/E2)

"I drink from the keg of glory, Donna. Bring me the finest muffins and bagels in all the land!"

~"Post Hoc, Ergo Propter Hoc" (s1/E2)

"Someone give me a river to forge, a serpent to slay."

~"Post Hoc, Ergo Propter Hoc" (s1/E2)

"I'm not gonna 'hide in my office.' I'm gonna go into my office and devise a strategy. That is what I do. I'm a professional. I'm not a little boy."

~"A Proportional Response" (s1/E3)

"Smallpox has been gone for 50 years. No one has an acquired immunity. Flies through the air. You get it... you carry a 10-foot cloud around with you. One in three people die. If 100 people in New York City got it, you'd have to encircle them with 100 million vaccinated people to contain it. Do you know how many doses of smallpox vaccines exist in the country? Seven. If 100 people in New York City get it, there's gonna be a global medical emergency that's gonna make HIV look like cold and flu season. That's how it's gonna be, a little test tube with a-a rubber cap that's deteriorating... A guy steps out of Times Square Station. Smashes it on the sidewalk... There's a world war right

there."
~ "The Crackpots and These Women" (S1/E5)

"Hi, Senator! Why don't you take your legislative agenda and shove it up your ass?"
~"Mandatory Minimums" (S1/E20)

"This is a place where solemn work is done. This is a place... this is a place... let me say this... this is not a place where one's personal things... where things among people... this is not a place... let's... This is a place where work is done and nothing else."
~"Mandatory Minimums" (S1/E20)

"You know what this is like? This is like *The Godfather*. When Pacino tells James Caan that he's gonna kill the cop. It's a lot like that scene, only not really."
~"Mandatory Minimums" (S1/E20)

"I need you to be done with dinner in an hour and five minutes. If you wanna have sex, you'd better do it during dinner."
~"The Portland Trip" (S2/E7)

"We can't just take him aside! If we tell him we need his help then we give him visibility and power, and we put him in a position to say 'no' and be a hero to his party! Who wouldn't want to do that for a living?
"You need to listen to me! You have to listen to me! I can't help you, unless you listen to me! You can't send Christmas cards to everyone, you can't do it! Forget the SPR, let's get the IMF loans like we said we were going to, listen to what I have to say about Didion, and please,

listen to me!"

~"Noël" (S2/E10)

"See, I think these are good people, by and large, but they've come under the thumb of a dictatorial ruler. So, as with a small, Central American country, my role is to incite the people to topple her."

~"The US Poet Laureate" (S3/E16)

"You know, there comes a day in every man's life, and it's a hard day, but there comes a day when he realizes he's never going to play professional baseball."

~"The Red Mass" (S4/E3)

"There's a reason why we keep these missile silos way out the hell in the middle nowhere! It's 'cause they're working with some pretty nasty materials! Also, there's not much point in keeping nuclear secrets from China when all they have to do is take the free [White House] tour. Did it really sound right to you, when he said it? What'd you think, we'd go to war, and Hercules rockets come flying out of the Rose Garden?"

~"Debate Camp" (S4/E4)

"I'm a fan. I'm a sports fan, I'm a music fan and I'm a *Star Trek* fan. All of them. But here's what I don't do. Tell me if any of this sounds familiar: 'Let's list our ten favorite episodes. Let's list our least favorite episodes. Let's list our favorite galaxies. Let's make a chart to see how often our favorite galaxies appear in our favorite episodes. What Romulan would you most like to see coupled with a Cardassian and why? Let's spend a weekend talking about Romulans falling in love with Cardassians and then let's do it again.' That's not being a fan. That's having a fetish. And I don't have a problem with that, except you can't bring your hobbies in to work, okay?"

~"Arctic Radar" (S4/E9)

"You know, I go for kiss-ass today and the ball goes in the gutter."

~"Guns Not Butter" (S4/E11)

"I got a letter today that said, 'You're a lying liar. You lie almost as well as Bartlet.' You know, black-white, rich-poor, north-south, odd-even. There may not be anything anymore that outpaces the hatred the right feels for the left or the tonnage of disrespect the left feels for the right. Donna got a letter yesterday that said, 'I'm collecting all the guns you've banned, and there's a bullet with your name on it in each one.' Donna. The guy's decided to focus his wrath on Donna! He's never met Donna or spoken to her, and he's never met anyone who's met Donna or spoken to her. How's it possible? How's it possible that he hates her so much? How can you not like Donna? She's from Wisconsin! Anyway, 20,000 specific threats made against US targets every year, and with all that, it's still the ones who don't give you advance notice that you're worried about."

~"Evidence of Things Not Seen" (S4/E19)

"I was the one who played sitar and made procedural changes."

~"Constituency of One" (S5/E5)

"Hey! You want a piece of me! I'm right here! I'm standing right here! Come on! Come on!"

~"Disaster Relief" (S5/E6)

"Children of your villages will sing my name!"

~"The Hubbert Peak" (S6/E5)

"Here's the part where in deference to my years of service, you suspend for a moment the Teutonic allegiance to protocol and shift thyself out of my way!"

~"Drought Conditions" (S6/E16)

thyself out of my way!"

~"Drought Conditions" (S6/E16)

Josh Lyman's Greatest Hits

"Why is it for every good thing you do around here, we've got to endure three screw-ups?" President Bartlet thunders at Josh in the Oval Office (in "We Killed Yamamoto"). Josh isn't getting enough votes on a welfare reauthorization bill, and he scheduled the vote in conflict with "The War of the Roses" charity benefit in New York, which the President is anxious to attend.

President Bartlet's ire may be justified, but his math is way off: day to day, Josh's balance of brainstorms and screw-ups is very well balanced:

- SCREW-UP: The Mary Marsh Mess. Josh disses the formidable Christian Right leader on live TV, putting the administration in a serious PR bind ("Pilot");
- BRAINSTORM: Big Sky National Park. Faced with a land use rider attached to a banking bill the administration really wants passed, a rider that will open up Big Sky Federal Reserve to strip-mining, Josh advises the President to declare the reserve a national park, thereby protecting it ("Enemies");
- SCREW-UP: The Secret Plan to Fight Inflation. Over-estimating his mastery of the Socratic wonder that is the White House Press Corps, Josh puts his foot in it and once again embarrasses himself and the administration by letting CJ's reporters tie him in knots ("Celestial Navigation");
- SCREW-UP: Giving Away Big Tobacco for Lunch Money. Incensed when he learns how lopsided the federal government's legal battles against Big Tobacco have become, he conspires to shame a vulnerable congressman into tipping a subcommittee's vote to provide more funding with a scathing press release; the money is released, but Josh has blown the chance to make it an issue for the re-elect ("Manchester, Pt. II");
- SCREW-UP: Party Switch. Surging with arrogance after a newspaper article praises his influence in Congress, Josh bullies Senator Chris Carrick of Idaho into releasing holds on military promotions; he may have been in the right, but his

ill-advised handling of Carrick results in the senator leaving the Democratic Party – imperiling the Bartlet White House's agenda in the Senate ("Constituency of One");

- BRAINSTORM: The Trip to the Hill. Badly burned over his Carrick mistake, Josh finds redemption in urging the President to go to the Hill to make amends with Speaker Haffley and end the government shutdown – and then doubles down, encouraging the President to *walk* there, for all the world to see, through the many news cameras ("Shutdown");

- BRAINSTORM: Leaving the Hill. That brainstorm is a two-fer, as Haffley and Majority Leader Royce, caught by surprise, stall to strategize and leave the President sitting on a bench in a hall before the cameras; "Let's go! Right now!" Josh ingeniously whispers; Haffley and Royce emerge to watch the President departing, as all the cameras follow ("Shutdown");

- BRAINSTORM: The Swappity-Doo. A picture of Donna's parents' two cats on a cookie tin inspires Josh to solve the problem of filling a seat on the Supreme Court with a mediocre moderate, when he wants the President to pick liberal firebrand Evelyn Baker Lang instead; he advises the President to put up Lang as Chief Justice, replacing the aging Roy Ashland, and getting her through confirmation by letting the Judiciary Committee pick whatever segregationist, anti-miscegenationist, Isaiah-quoting, gay-bashing bastard they please – which President Bartlet does, resulting in the first-ever appointment of a woman to Chief Justice ("The Supremes").

In our final tally, then, that's 4 brainstorms and 4 screw-ups (the Oval Office incident he was bawled out for doesn't register – in the end, the House passed the iffy welfare bill). We can safely say Josh is every bit as brilliant as he is stupid!

Character Quizzes

Jed Bartlet

See how much you know about Jed Bartlet:

1. What is Jed Bartlet's actual first name?
2. What is his brother's name?
3. Why did President Bartlet go to Notre Dame?
4. Why didn't he pursue his original goal?
5. What vegetable doesn't he like?
6. What is his favorite movie?

Leo McGarry

See how much you know about Leo McGarry:

1. What is Leo's middle name?
2. What city is he from?
3. In what branch of the military did he serve?
4. Where did he go to school?
5. He was treated for addiction to alcohol and Valium in 1993. Where?
6. He served in a previous Presidential cabinet. As what?

Josh Lyman

See how much you know about Josh Lyman:

1. What is Josh's father's name and profession?
2. Where did he do his undergrad studies? His law studies?
3. In law school, he earned a prestigious academic status. What was it?
4. His sister died when he was a child. What was her name?
5. How did she die?
6. What sport did he dream of playing professionally?

CJ Cregg

See how much you know about CJ Cregg:

1. Where is CJ from?
2. How many siblings does she have?
3. She achieved distinction in sports in her youth. What did she do?
4. Where did she attend college and grad school?
5. She has a master's degree in what subject?
6. What was her salary at Triton Day when Leo sent Toby to recruit her for the Bartlet campaign?

Toby Ziegler

See how much you know about Toby Ziegler:

1. Where was Toby born and raised?
2. What is his full name?
3. Besides his brother David, what siblings does he have?
4. How many Yankee games has he attended, on the occasion that he speaks of it?
5. He was raised on three public television classics. What were they?
6. How old did one of his grandfathers live to be?

Sam Seaborn

See how much you know about Sam Seaborn:

1. Where did Sam grow up?
2. What summer camp did he attend as a boy?
3. Where did he go to school (undergrad and law?
4. What organization did he serve as recording secretary in college?
5. What journal did he edit while in law school?
6. In what foreign language is he fluent?

Abbey Bartlet

See how much you know about Abbey Bartlet:

1.   Where did she earn her undergraduate degree?
2.   Where did she earn her MD?
3.   In what medical disciplines is she board-certified?
4.   At what medical school is she an adjunct professor?
5.   How many generations back was her DAR-qualifying relative?
6.   For what other West Wing character did Abbey once babysit?

Charlie Young

See how much you know about Charlie Young:

1.   What is Charlie's younger sister's name?
2.   Where did he attend high school?
3.   Where did he take his college classes?
4.   He originally applies for a position at the White House other than the President's body man. What position?
5.   What movie franchise does Charlie love, from which the President gifts him a DVD, and what is the DVD?
6.   Charlie is like a son to the President, who gives him a family heirloom as a gift one Thanksgiving. What is it?

Donna Moss

See how much you know about Donna Moss:

1.   What is Donna's actual first name?
2.   Where was she born?
3.   Where was she raised?
4.   To whom did she lose her virginity, and how old was she?
5.   Where did she attend college?
6.   In what state does she have family, other than her relatives in Wisconsin?

Mrs. Landingham

See how much you know about Mrs. Landingham:

1. What is Mrs. Landingham's first name?
2. What was her husband's name?
3. What is her position when Jed Bartlet meets her for the first time?
4. What are the names of her twin sons?
5. What became of her sons?
6. She treated Charlie like a nephew, and at her funeral, he gives a reading. What is the reading from?

Will Bailey

See how much you know about Will Bailey:

1. We can guess at the school Will attended from the shirt he's wearing while jogging at Camp David. What school is the shirt from?
2. While running, Will calls out that he only has the legs to run what distance?
3. Where did he go to grad school, and on what scholarship?
4. While in grad school, he was president of what student group?
5. He was a speechwriter for a state-level politician who also appeared on *The West Wing*. Who?
6. Will is an Air Force reserve officer. Who does he work for, in the Air Force?

Character Quiz Answers

Jed Bartlet
1. Josiah
2. John
3. He was thinking of becoming a priest
4. He met Abbey
5. Green beans
6. *The Lion in Winter*

Leo McGarry
1. Thomas
2. Chicago
3. The US Air Force
4. University of Michigan
5. Sierra-Tucson
6. Secretary of Labor

Josh Lyman
1. Noah; attorney (litigator and partner at Debevoise and Plimpton)
2. Harvard; Yale
3. He was a Fulbright Scholar
4. Joanie
5. She was trapped in their burning home (Josh, who was younger, escaped)
6. baseball

CJ Cregg
1. Dayton, Ohio
2. two older brothers
3. first female player in Ohio high school history to dunk a basketball
4. Williams College; UC Berkeley
5. Political Science

6. $550,000/yr

Toby Ziegler
1. Brighton Beach, Brooklyn
2. Tobias Zachary Ziegler
3. An undetermined number of older sisters
4. 441
5. *Sesame Street*, *Julia Child*, and *Brideshead Revisited*
6. 96

Sam Seaborn
1. Laguna Beach, California
2. Dungeons & Dragons camp
3. Princeton; Duke
4. The Princeton Gilbert & Sullivan Society
5. The *Duke Law Review*
6. Spanish

Abbey Bartlet
1. St. Mary's College (conjecture; she met Jed Bartlet while he was attending Notre Dame, but it wasn't yet co-ed; St. Mary's was Notre Dame's nearby sister institution)
2. Harvard
3. Internal Medicine; Thoracic Surgery
4. Harvard Medical School
5. 17
6. Amy Gardner

Charlie Young
1. Deana
2. Roosevelt High, in Washington, DC
3. Georgetown University
4. part-time messenger
5. James Bond; *On Her Majesty's Secret Service*

6. a set of carving knives made by Boston silversmith Paul Revere

Donna Moss

1. Donnatella
2. Warroad, Minnesota
3. Madison, Wisconsin
4. Freddy Briggs; 16
5. University of Wisconsin
6. Oklahoma

Mrs. Landingham

1. Dolores
2. Henry
3. secretary to Jed Bartlet's father at the prep school where he was headmaster
4. Andrew and Simon
5. They were killed in a firefight in Da Nang, Vietnam, on Christmas Day, 1970
6. *The Book of Wisdom*

Will Bailey

1. Carnegie Mellon
2. 5 miles
3. Cambridge; a Marshall Scholarship
4. The Cambridge Union Society
5. California Gov. Gabriel Tillman
6. JAG (Judge Advocate General) Corps

The Top 10 CJ Moments

Of all the major players on the Bartlet White House stage, no one changes over the course of the Bartlet Presidency than CJ Cregg. She goes from novice press secretary to Leo McGarry's successor before our eyes, as she weathers challenges from within and without, manages scandal, engages in her own back-room activism, and suffers tragic loss – emerging as a strong and brilliant leader in her own right.

Here are some of the best moments from those years:

"I just wish I didn't know his mother's name was Sophia, is all I'm saying."

In one of the Bartlet Administration's first true it's-getting-real moments, a murderous drug lord is about to be executed, and the President wrestles with whether or not to stay the execution. He doesn't, despite the efforts of Sam and Toby to encourage him to do so.

And it falls to CJ to be the bearer of the news of the drug lord's death on the night of the execution. In a spontaneous from-the-heart confession to Mandy, she declares that she has no real position on capital punishment, and that she doesn't really care about the fate of Simon Cruz. She then proceeds to describe what actually transpires in the course of the execution, reading from prepared materials, and notes the actions she herself will take, by way of informing the President. Her summation of all this, talking to Mandy, strongly suggests that it's one thing to have no position when none is required; but it's something else altogether when the reality of what's happening requires a moral response:

"I have to go in and tell the President that Simon Cruz is dead, and we're the ones who killed him. So. I just wish I didn't know his mother's name was Sophia, is all I'm saying."

"...the most powerful lesbian on the planet..."

Not long after her appointment as Chief of Staff, CJ is forced to confront rumors in the press that she is, in fact, a closeted lesbian (in "Faith Based Initiative"). This is upsetting on several levels, not least the balancing act she must now put herself through in order to cope with the behaviors of those indulging in the gossip and her own moral convictions about the right to privacy to which she and all the people nattering about her should be entitled. And she must deal with all this while still getting her bearings in her new role.

In a funny and beautiful scene in her old office, she spontaneously unloads all of this on a hapless Leo, serving up not only her feelings about her problem but also a host of other personal issues – her past and recent romantic disappointments, her ancient insecurities, her disillusionment over the expectations of others - Leo is, to say the least, caught in headlights:

"...now, I'm looking at some bad numbers, really rough stuff, if you know what I'm talking about. But what was I supposed to do? Turn down an opportunity to serve the President of the United States whom I believe in and adore? You just want to share it all with someone, you know?"

"The President of the United States himself
was shot last night while surrounded by the best-trained
armed guards in the history of the world."

In the aftermath of the Rosslyn shooting, in one of a long series of difficult press conferences, CJ makes a spontaneous amendment to her update on the condition of the President and Josh Lyman, both of whom were wounded. She offers a list of ordinary Americans who were likewise injured by guns on the same night, then offers statistics about other gun-related crimes that occurred across the nation. She is, in effect, reminding the press corps (and Leo and Danny Concannon, watching from the back of the room) that the problem of gun violence is by no means limited to the shooting of the President:

"And if anyone thinks those crimes could have been prevented if the victims themselves had been carrying guns, I'd only remind you that the President of the United States himself was shot last night while surrounded by the best trained armed guards in the history of the world."

"She's good," Danny whispers.

"Yes, she is!" Leo agrees.

"This cancels a good and valuable life!"

As her father is succumbing to the shadows of dementia, his wife – CJ's stepmother – has abandoned him, but he hasn't told her. When she returns to Dayton to deliver a high school union speech, she learns the truth, and seeks out her stepmother for a confrontation.

"What happened to reciprocity? Do you ever imagine in a million years if the roles were reversed, he would ever do this to you? This is - what you're doing, right now! - invalidates everything that came before all the good, the years of teaching. This cancels a good and valuable life! He needs you!"

This speech, this dressing-down, is more than a loving but exhausted daughter's defense of an increasingly defenseless father; it is CJ's moral stand, not just in the situation, but the broader landscape of her role as public servant. It's about *what we owe each other*, the ethical bonds of humanity, convictions that lie even deeper within her than familial love.

"If America's choices are going to be restricted, so are yours!"

When an FCC ruling empowering media monopolies is announced, CJ is incensed at its transparent kowtowing to elites and the brazen reduction of barriers to private control of the media. She appeals to her press corps reporters, encouraging them to expose this blatant blow to free speech – and is rebuffed; none of them wants to be in the position of writing critical articles about their bosses.

So she takes matters into her own hands, and undertakes the drastic step of gutting the seats in the press room – leaving one each for a representative of each of the seven conglomerates controlling the media: "I guess you'll have to flip a coin to see who gets to sit!

"If America's choices are going to be restricted, so are yours, and everyone's gonna know it," she tells them. This can't last, of course, it's only a gesture; but it's a gesture that clarifies CJ as a woman whose values aren't arbitrary. If she sees a wrong that needs righting, she'll cajole whoever she needs to get it righted.

Leo, impressed with her conviction and her willingness to ruffle feathers in defense of it, offers to reimburse her for the carpentry. She politely refuses.

"Thanks, but it was worth every nickel!"

"I like that you're tall..."

Threatened by a stalker, CJ finds herself involuntarily under Secret Service protection, led by Simon Donovan, with whom she becomes smitten. We're not used to this at all; CJ typically presents as not easily impressed with men, and over-willing to inform us how good in bed she is – an alpha, in other words.

With Donovan, it's different, despite her efforts to put a wall between them. Their flirtation is so ridden with dry wit and exasperation that it makes their obvious attraction to each other all the more endearing.

The shining moment in their relationship happens at the Treasury Department's gymnasium, where CJ has a workout and Donovan gives her a quick session of target practice with a handgun. A wager is made: If Donovan can bulls-eye three shots, she will be required to say something nice about him – something she was resisted doing.

He lands not three, but five. She has to pay up:

"I like that you're tall," she says, with almost meek girlishness. "It makes me feel more feminine."

This is an astonishing moment, tender and out-of-the-blue, with CJ coming across as awkward and vulnerable – light-years away from her loud declaration to Tad Whitney, later reiterated in the Oval Office in front of the President, "I am *great* in bed!"

In this moment, we love her a little more.

"It's about going to the blackboard and raising your hand!"

The President is preparing to host an educational broadcast to 60,000 public school students on the occasion of the landing of the *Galileo* probe on Mars. Excited by the opportunity to reach out to so many young people, he tasks CJ and Sam with coming up with a larger theme for the event.

Then the *Galileo*'s signal is lost, and it looks as though the event will be canceled. But CJ encourages the President to see it through, signal or no signal, in a beautiful exchange on the Colonnade outside the Oval Office in the evening air: in one of her most idealistic turns, she expresses that the entire point of endeavors like the Galileo mission is taking risks in order to learn, and that this should be something everyone does – not just NASA scientists:

"We have, at our disposal, a captive audience of schoolchildren. Some of them don't go to the black board and raise their hand 'cause they think they're gonna be wrong. I think you should say to these kids, 'You think you get it wrong sometimes? You should come down here and see how the big boys do it!

"Some of them will laugh, and most of them won't care, but for some, they might honestly see that it's about going to the blackboard and raising your hand!"

"Frank Hollis wants me to take ten billion dollars and go and fix the world..."

As the Bartlet Administration is ending, CJ has two big decisions looming: what to do with her life now, and what future she might have with Danny Concannon. Two scenes bookend this moment in her life and career: an offer from tech billionaire Frank Hollis to appoint her as executive director of his new foundation, and a confrontation with Danny over how he fits into her at-loose-ends direction.

This is one of CJ's best moments in the series. It's the perfect culmination of her seven-season relationship with Danny – and, of course, the massive career shift when she was deservedly elevated to Chief of Staff, opening up a new world of potential and opportunity. Both she and Danny are superb, as he seeks to offer calm and support as she thrashes through the uncertainties of possibilities she never dreamed she have.

Danny cuts through it all in 10 seconds:

"[Taking $10 billion and fixing the world] sounds like fun! Does that sound like fun to you?" She nods.

"Do you wanna work at the White House?" She shakes her head.

As beautiful as that exchange is, it is topped by Danny's

proclamation of his own thoughts about their uncertain future:

"I want us to talk about what it'll mean and how we'll make it work! I want us to talk like we're gonna figure it out together! I want us to talk – because I like the sound of your voice!"

"You're really very sweet sometimes. You really are!"

Josh Lyman is crafty, relentless, and formidable – a tough combatant in the Washington arena. So when he gets instructions on where to go in case of a nuclear attack, it's a bit of a downshift to see his hesitation – that he would survive such an attack while his friends wouldn't is more than he can bear.

It is CJ to whom he chooses to unburden himself of this feeling. When she comes to his office to urge him to head for the chili supper in the residence, he blurts it all out:

"They want me up in the plane or down on a bunker! They don't want you - or Sam, or Toby, for that matter. I didn't want to be friends with you and have you not know."

His honesty and agony touch her deeply, and she offers him an assurance that demonstrates that she is a friend worthy of such devotion:

"You're really very sweet sometimes. You really are!" She gives him a smile that expresses how much she appreciates the genuineness of the moment.

"Come have chili. The President's asking for you!"

"Tonight, I've seen a man with no legs keep standing, Dad, and a man with no voice keep shouting..."

CJ serves as narrator of one of *The West Wing*'s all-time greatest stories – the aging Senator Howard Stackhouse taking the Senate hostage, stalling a vote on a family healthcare bill. In an email to her own aging and ailing father that evening, which also happens to be his 70th birthday, she expresses her annoyance and that of the senior staff (likewise held hostage) over the stubborn senator's filibuster, which is inconveniencing hundreds of people.

Donna Moss figures out what's going on: Stackhouse is holding up the healthcare bill to attach a rider that will fund autism research, as he makes clear to Josh; but he's doing it because he has an autistic grandson, which he didn't tell anybody.

Realizing that the senator's filibuster isn't political grandstanding, but rather a desperate gesture to extend the bill's funding power to children who often go unnoticed, the Bartlet team go into high gear - rallying other senators to return to the Senate floor to help Stackhouse get over the finish line so the vote can be set aside until the bill is amended.

The power of the final scene is CJ's unabashed awe at the goodness of what Stackhouse has done, and the lack of hesitation in so many to help him.

"...and if politics brings out the worst in people, then maybe people bring out the best – 'cause I'm looking at the TV right now and damned if 28 US Senators haven't just walked onto the floor to help!"

~TWW~

The Other Side of the Camera

Brad Whitford contributed two scripts to *The West Wing*: "Faith Based Initiative" (S6/E10) and "Internal Displacement" (S7/E11).

Richard Schiff directed two episodes: "Talking Points" (S5/E19) and "A Good Day" (S6/E17).

Tim Matheson (Vice President John Hoynes) directed an episode: "The Last Hurrah" (S7/E20)

...and in the other direction, writer Lawrence O'Donnell, who penned (or co-penned) 16 episodes, went in front of the camera to play Jed Bartlet's father in "Two Cathedrals" (S2/E22).

~TWW~

When Josh's plane is called at the airport as he talks with Gov. Bartlet in the flashback scene in "In the Shadow of Two Gunmen, Pt. II", the voice calling it is Martin Sheen's.

The Best of CJ Cregg

"This is our 5th press briefing since midnight. Obviously, there's one story that going dominating news around the world for the next few days, and it would be easy to think that President Bartlet, Joshua Lyman, and Stephanie Abbott were the only victims of a gun crime last night. They weren't. Mark Davis and Sheila Evans of Philadelphia were killed by a gun last night. He was a biology teacher and she was a nursing student. Tina Bishop and Linda Larkin were killed with a gun last night. They were 12. There were 36 homicides last night. 480 sexual assaults, 3,411 robberies, 3,685 aggravated assaults, all at gunpoint. And if anyone thinks those crimes could have been prevented if the victims themselves had been carrying guns, I'd only remind you that the President of the United States himself was shot last night while surrounded by the best trained armed guards in the history of the world."

~ "In the Shadow of Two Gunmen, Pt. II" (S2/E2)

"You leaked it for me, I leaked it to you, pal! I used you like so much whatever."

~"The Lame Duck Congress" (S2/E6)

"We have, at our disposal, a captive audience of schoolchildren. Some of them don't go to the blackboard and raise their hand 'cause they think they're gonna be wrong. I think you should say to these kids, you think you get it wrong sometimes? You should come down here and see how the big boys do it! I think you should tell them you haven't given up hope, and that it may turn up, but in the meantime, you want NASA to put its best people in the room, and you want them to start building *Galileo VI*. Some of them will laugh, and most of them won't care, but for some, they might honestly see that it's about going to the blackboard and raising your hand."

~"Galileo" (S2/E9)

"I'm the enforcer, Sam! I'm gonna crush him, I'm gonna make him cry, and then I'm gonna tell his momma about it!"

~"Ellie" (S2/E15)

"Tonight I've seen a man with no legs keep standing, Dad, and a guy with no voice keep shouting, and if politics brings out the worst in people, then maybe people bring out the best – 'cause I'm looking at the TV right now, and damned if 28 US Senators haven't just walked onto the floor to help. I'll catch the first plane out in the morning, and if you wouldn't mind not turning 70 until tomorrow, that'd be great. In the meantime, I love you so much! Your daughter, Claudia."

~"The Stackhouse Filibuster" (S2/E17)

"It's not like I have instant recall of every ceramic cat statue I've ever been handed in Cairo!"

~"The Stackhouse Filibuster" (S2/E17)

"You guys are like Butch and Sundance peering over the edge of a cliff to the boulder-filled rapids 300 feet below, thinking you better not jump 'cause there's a chance you might drown. The President has this disease and has been lying about it, and you guys are worried that the polling might make us look bad? It's the fall that's gonna kill ya!"

~"The Fall's Gonna Kill You" (S2/E20)

"Leo, we need to be investigated by someone who wants to kill us just to watch us die! We need someone perceived by the American people to be irresponsible, untrustworthy, partisan, ambitious and thirsty for the limelight. Am I crazy or is this not a job for the US House

of Representatives?"
~"Ways and Means" (S3/E3)

"I don't know, sir. When I came in here, back in the late Fifties, there was a purpose to it, but then one thing led to another and I blacked out. I mean, I can hang in there with the best of them, sir, but somewhere during the discussion of anise and coriander and the other 15 spices you like to use to baste a turkey, I simply lost consciousness."
~"The Indians in the Lobby" (S3/E7)

"The cow made of butter? That's how I like my irony served, my friend."
~"The Two Bartlets" (S3/E12)

"Okay, Secret Agent Man, here's my rules and regulations! I'm getting in my baby blue '65 Mustang convertible and I'm gonna feel the wind in my hair and any place else I want. You can look at my taillights!"
~"The Black Vera Wang" (S3/E19)

"What girl can resist being referred to as poultry?"
~"The Warfare of Genghis Khan" (S5/E13)

"No, the President has no intention of starting a worldwide bra war. I really don't think the President would ever start a war that the French might actually win."
~"Full Disclosure" (S5/E15)

"When you run for President, the press is going to find some of those women. And if you try to attack them, if you get your opposition research team working on them, if you try to destroy them, if you try to say they're all bimbos and liars, then I'll be standing right there with them and I'll be ready to take anything you or your people throw at me, anything.

"So don't make me tell the truth about you, because it will be the *whole* truth."

~"Full Disclosure" (S5/E15)

"'Gee, CJ, I'm sorry your boss and dear friend is sprawled across an operating table having his veins harvested, but I do think it's kind of neat the President single-handedly forged a major peace deal. Why don't I write about it until my typewriter's tangled up in ribbon?'"

~"Third Day Story" (S6/E3)

"You're an odd woman, and I've never quite understood you. But you are extremely capable, and you run this office like a Swiss watch, and you're tall, which is reassuring. Leo may need you and if he does, that's okay. But if he's willing to part with you, I hope you'll stay."

~to Margaret, "Liftoff" (S6/E4)

"I'm a heterosexual, and I don't know why I just said that, except that as of this morning, I'm the most famous, not famous, but apparently the most powerful lesbian on the planet, when the fact of the matter is I'm crazy, absolutely crazy about this particular man I just met and had two fabulous dinners with in the space of one week, a man who hasn't had the courtesy to call me today, probably because he is simply of the undependable gender, or, come to think of it, maybe he has even less of an idea about how to deal with my alleged and fictitious lesbianism than I do. So, he'll just remain silent, like a submarine under the ice cap and drift away, just drift away like the legion of other cowards for whom I spent my young life staring at the phone, panting like an exquisite collie hoping for table scraps. Until I became successful, and suddenly started to scare them, scare them with the very independence they required me to have, so that now, I'm looking at some bad numbers, really rough stuff, if you know what I'm talking about. But what was I supposed to do? Turn down an opportunity to serve the President of the United States whom I believe

in and adore? You just want to share it all with someone, you know?"
~"Faith Based Initiative" (S6/E10)

"Can't you see that I'm losing my mind? And if I can't sleep, I need at least 10 minutes of quiet time to myself. Quiet time. My time! I'm going out to get coffee. I'm learning to freebase the stuff, if that's what it takes to make this life livable: peace and quiet, and an IV of caffeine. Can I get you anything?"
~"Mr. Frost" (S7/E4)

"[The press] ticked me off because they care more about coming up with a good story than they do about telling the truth! So now I have to live in a culture where what's important doesn't matter, because we're too preoccupied by people who are more attractive than we are playing musical genitalia in Hollywood!"
~"Internal Displacement" (S7/E11)

"I feel like I'm the heroine in the movie who doesn't know there's a guy behind the refrigerator with an axe."
~"The Cold" (S7/E13)

"You spend your whole life working for powerful, demanding men 24/7! That's a lot of testosterone in your world. Wow, maybe you didn't need to date! You had Josh and Sam and me and 180 reporters flirting with you day in and day out! That's a lot of positive male attention. Now you're sliding in Matt Santos, maybe Frank Hollis?

"You showed up here at 8:00 at night with a bottle of wine, asking me about a pardon we both know is out of the question, telling me about a man who's crowding you. I think a lot of things. I think you don't know why you came here tonight. You're a woman with a lot of options. You're acting like the world's backing you into a corner, bouncing from one thing to the next, from Bartlet to Santos to Danny to me? Maybe you should stop bouncing, pick something.

"What do you want?"
~to CJ, "Institutional Memory" (S7/E21)

The Top 25 Episode Lists

At this writing, in the fall of 2024, *The West Wing* is celebrating its 25th birthday – and many entertainment publications are serving up Top 25 lists of the best West Wing episodes.

Here are some of the most prominent. It's interesting to see where they agree...

Variety

25 "The Supremes" (S5/E17)

24 "Celestial Navigation" (S1/E15)

23 "The Debate" (S7/E7)

21 "Life on Mars" (S4/E21)

21 "Duck and Cover" (S7/E12)

20 "Process Stories" (S4/E8)

19 "Posse Comitatus" (S3/E21)

18 "In the Room" (S6/E8)

17 "Manchester" (S3/E1,2)

16 "What Kind of Day Has It Been" (S1/E22)

15 "Somebody's Going to Emergency,
Somebody's Going to Jail" (S2/E16)

14 "In This White House" (S2/E4)

13 "Pilot", S1/E1)

12 "Hartsfield's Landing" (S3/E14)

11 "Shibboleth" (S2/E8)

10 "Twenty Five" (S4/E23)

9 "Dead Irish Writers" (S3/E15)

8 "In Excelsis Deo" (S1/E10)

7 "Bartlet for America" (S3/E9)

6 "17 People" (S2/E18)

5 "20 Hours in America" (S4/E1,2)

4 "Let Bartlet Be Bartlet" (S1/E19)

3 "Noël" (S2/E10)

2 "In the Shadow of Two Gunmen" (S2/E1,2)

1 "Two Cathedrals" (S2/E22)

Not a bad list at all! We expect to see most of these on *any* Top 25 list – the Emmy-winning "In Excelsis Deo", "Bartlet for America", "17 People", "In the Shadow of Two Gunmen", "20 Hours in America", "Twenty Five" – and, of course, "Two Cathedrals" at #1. "Two Cathedrals" is a masterpiece, and is almost *always* at #1.

As with most such lists, there are a few episodes missing that we usually see – "The Stackhouse Filibuster" and "And It's Surely to Their Credit" spring to mind – and a couple are on the list that we usually *don't* see ("Process Stories", "Duck and Cover").

Then there are the episodes that fall higher or lower on the list than we might expect; "Posse Comitatus" is too low? "Dead Irish Writers" is too high?

Still, we're moving in the direction of an overlapping consensus.

IMDB

25 "Talking Points"

24 "The Midterms"

23 "2162 Votes"

22 "Election Day, Pt. II"

21 "The Crackpots and These Women"

20 "Posse Comitatus" (S3/E21)

19 "He Shall, from Time to Time..."

18 "No Exit"

17 "Tomorrow"

16 "Slow News Day"

15 "Shutdown"

14 "Dead Irish Writers" (S3/E15)

13 "In This White House" (S2/E4)

12 "Somebody's Going to Emergency,
Somebody's Going to Jail"

11 "And It's Surely to Their Credit"

10 "Evidence of Things Not Seen"

9 "Twenty Five" (S4/E23)

8 "Requiem"

7 "Bartlet for America" (S3/E9)

6 "In the Shadow of Two Gunmen, Pt. I" (S2/E1)

5 "The Stackhouse Filibuster"

4 "In Excelsis Deo" (S1/E10)

3 "The Supremes" (S5/E17)

2 "20 Hours in America, Pt. II" (S4/E2)

1 "Two Cathedrals" (S2/E22)

Again, there are a few episodes on the list that don't normally appear ("Talking Points", "The Crackpots and These Women") and a couple we'd expect to see, but don't ("Noël", "17 People", "Let Bartlet Be Bartlet"). Again, some seem to land too low ("Posse Comitatus") while others sit too high ("Evidence of Things Not Seen").

And, as we'd expect, "Two Cathedrals" is the top pick.

Stacker

25 "Mr. Willis of Ohio" (S1/E6)

24 "Pilot" (S1/E1)

23 "20 Hours in America, Pt. II" (S4/E2)

22 "2162 Votes" (S6/E22)

21 "Requiem" (S7/E18)

20 "17 People" (S2/E18)

19 "Tomorrow" (S7/E22)

18 "The Stackhouse Filibuster" (S2/E17)

17 "Take This Sabbath Day" (S1/E14)

16 "Game On" (S4/E6)

15 "Commencement" (S4/E22)

14 "18th and Potomac" (S2/E21)

13 "Let Bartlet Be Bartlet" (S1/E19)

12 "Celestial Navigation" (S1/E15)

11 "Election Day, Pt. II" (S7/E17)

10 "Bartlet for America" (S3/E9)

9 "The Supremes" (S5/E17)

8 "Posse Comitatus" (S3/E22)

7   "In Excelsis Deo" (S1/E10)

6 "What Kind of Day Has It Been" (S1/E22)

5 "Twenty Five" (S4/E23)

4 "In the Shadow of Two Gunmen, Pt. II" (S2/E2)

3 "Noël" (S2/E10)

2 "In the Shadow of Two Gunmen, Pt. I" (S2/E1)

1 "Two Cathedrals" (S2/E22"

Why "2162 Votes"? Why "Mr. Willis of Ohio"? And where's Ainsley? Neither "In This White House" nor "And It's Surely to Their Credit" made this list. And where's "Somebody's Going to Emergency, Somebody's Going to Jail?"

We can quibble over the low positions of "17 People" and "The Stackhouse Filibuster", and the high positions of "Twenty Five" and "Election Day, Pt. II" – but as long as "Two Cathedrals" remains on top, we are still inclined to consider this list legitimate.

As for our emerging consensus, we note the following episodes on all three lists (weighted by their average positions):

Two Cathedrals
In the Shadow of Two Gunmen
Bartlet for America
Twenty Five
In Excelsis Deo
20 Hours in America
The Supremes
Posse Comitatus

...and among these, the following fall into the Top 10 on all three lists:

Two Cathedrals
In the Shadow of Two Gunmen
Bartlet for America
Twenty Five
In Excelsis Deo

Can we call these the Top 5?

We can note with surprise that some very popular fan favorites only made one of these lists ("Noel", "Take This Sabbath Day") – but it's all subjective, of course.

What are your Top 25?

The *West Wing* Library!

Victim to My Own Purity of Character, by Josiah Bartlet

Drinking from the Keg of Glory, by Josh Lyman

Claudia's House of Useless Knowledge, by CJ Cregg

A Smudge of Law, by Toby Ziegler

Bad on So Many Levels, by Sam Seaborn

*Running as Fast as I Possibly Can and
Other Self-Defense Tips*,
by Charlie Young

The Grumpy Man's Wit, by Dolores Landingham

I've Got a Pretty Good-Looking Resume, by Oliver Babish

An Enemy I Can Kill, by Adm. Percy Fitzwallace

I'm Not 100% Sure I Was Supposed to Know That,
by Danny Concannon

Rubes Throw Down, by Annabeth Schott

I Know the Way Out, by Leo McGarry

A Man of Occasion, by Josh Lyman

I Lent Voice to Thought, by Toby Ziegler

20-30 Recipes, by CJ Cregg

Cunning & Guile, by Sam Seaborn

~TWW~

Josh often makes much of the number of White House employees – 1,100 – but in fact it's three times that many.

~TWW~

Former FLOTUS mentioned on *The West Wing*:

- Abigail Adams ("Ninety Miles Away")
- Dolley Madison ("Noel")
- Edith Wilson ("Bartlet for America")
- Eleanor Roosevelt ("The Women of Qumar")
- Bess Truman ("Five Votes Down")

Edith Wilson is likewise invoked elsewhere in the Sorkinverse, in *The American President* when Andrew Shepherd is trying to justify his dating Sydney Ellen Wade.

~TWW~

Former real-world White House staffers mentioned on TWW:

- Wilton Persons, Eisenhower Chief of Staff ("The Short List")
- Arthur Schlesinger, Jr., Special Assistant to JFK ("The Short List")
- Ted Sorenson, White House Counsel to JFK and LBJ ("The Short List")

The Top 10 Toby Moments

Then there's Toby. His wonderful moments generally present those depths we don't see up close on a normal workday. In extraordinary circumstances, we see the kinda-dark, kinda-cold Toby as a man with a warm and glowing heart...

"I wanted to be standing right next to you..."

As prickly and dour as Toby Ziegler generally is, day-to-day, he is nonetheless a big-hearted, fully-invested friend and colleague. Like so many who inhabit the Bartlet White House, he will march through the desert for a cause he believes in or a crusader needing support.

His deputy Sam Seaborn is one of them. As Sam follows through on an ill-advised promise made to a widow back in his home county, running for the House in the California 47th, Toby honors his friend's effort by taking charge of his campaign. It's a forlorn effort; he stands no chance of winning in such a heavily right-wing district (in "Red Haven's on Fire").

"You're gonna lose, and you're gonna lose huge," Toby admits. "They're gonna throw rocks at you next week, and I wanted to be standing next to you when they did."

"No, it doesn't, Mr. President..."

When Toby's brother David is stranded in space thanks to a glitch in the Space Shuttle, Toby finds himself emotionally vulnerable as he is overwhelmed with worry for his brother while his colleagues monitor the situation. President Bartlet himself approaches Toby to express support – poignant, as the two aren't getting along so well.

In typical Toby fashion, he manages to be appreciative and awkwardly blunt at the same time, reflecting his uncompromising honesty and lack of deference to niceties. This is a scene that definitely showcases who Toby really is (in "What Kind of Day Has It Been?"):

"Mr. President, I appreciate you trying to be a comfort, and I appreciate that you have some understanding of the situation with my brother - but the thing was supposed to land 19 hours ago. Obviously, there's a problem. It's space travel, and I don't believe any problem is minor."

"The Shuttle flies itself, Toby."

"No, it doesn't, Mr. President..."

"Do not, do not, DO NOT act like it!"

Toby's directness and seeming lack of filters where his boss is concerned takes a very emphatic turn as the Bartlet team comes to terms with the upcoming re-election contest, noting the challenge of the Republican chosen to oppose him. Toby confronts the President very directly as they sit in the Oval Office playing chess, and Bartlet waffles about how best to present himself during the campaign (in "Hartsfield's Landing). What Toby says to him comes across as urgent, critical, and admiring, all at the same time:

"You're a good father, you don't have to act like it! You're the President, you don't have to act like it! You're a good man, you don't have to act like it! You're not 'just folks', you're not plain-spoken -. Do not, do not, *do not* act like it!"

"It's a salad! Do I have to know the names?"

Intent on restoring his relationship with his ex-wife Andy, Toby undertakes to modify the behaviors she has found concerning in the past – including his diet. To this end, he is eating better, which only makes him more irritable. In a moment both revealing and hilarious, he erupts with frustration, as Charlie looks on (in "Life on Mars"):

"I don't know what kind of salad it is! I'm eating a salad, okay? I'm doing it. Do I have to know the names? There's no difference between them. It's a bowl of weeds! Some of them have cheese. This isn't the kind with cheese. Does that answer your question? How many years have you guys been, 'Toby, you eat like a teenager!' 'Toby, that's red meat!' 'That's your second cigar!' Here I am eating a salad, which, by the way, you could cover this thing in barbecue sauce and it would *still* taste like the ground, and I'm getting heckled from the gallery, who wanted to come in here to eat his roast beef sandwich with ketchup on a kaiser roll and watch the damn tennis on my TV! That's all I'm saying."

"Did my friends feel that way?"

We see Toby at his most vulnerable in "Commencement", as he takes Andy to a house he has bought for the two of them, hoping desperately for their remarriage. It is a scene that leaves him more emotionally exposed than we've ever seen him, as he grapples with her rejection in the face of the most self-sacrificing gesture he could conceive. Her own frustration with the situation bubbles up, exacerbated by her pregnancy (she is carrying twins), and she lets loose with some comments – "You're just too sad for me! You're sad, and you're angry, and you're not warm!" – and he is devastated. Understanding how her words must be bludgeoning him, we ache for him, and the scene is difficult to watch.

As her outburst subsides, his voice is unimaginably small as he asks, through his embarrassment, "Did my friends feel like that?"

"I like what's important to me! I want it to stay important!"

His new fatherhood causes Toby anxiety, and after his encounter with Andy and the birth of his twins, he confides in Leo – who likewise has crashed and burned in the domestic realm.

It is a moment of rare candor and sharing of intimate concerns, as Toby confesses his anxiety – a tension between his ability to be the kind of father the world expects him to be, and remaining true to the core values he has spent a lifetime crafting and nurturing. It's another definitive scene that shows who Toby really is:[22]

"If, for nine months, you're hearing how this is gonna change your life, and: 'You've never loved anything like this!' and, 'My God, the love!' and, 'Nothing's gonna be important anymore!' It just never really felt to me like I was someone who had the capacity for those feelings.

---

[22] In "Twenty Five".

Plus, you know, I *like* what's important to me! I want it to stay important!"

Leo assures him he'll be a great dad, and yet remain the committed man he is. "It's a mortal lock!"

"Babies come with hats!"

Toby's concerns about the father he'll be rapidly dissipate in a private moment in the hospital with his new son and daughter, just after their birth. He talks to the two of them, lying on a hospital bed, explaining with no self-consciousness just who he is and how he will fit into their lives. It's hard to imagine a more warm-hearted, endearing scene, or one that shows the depth of love Toby is capable of:

"So, what do I do? Well, you're gonna need food and clothes and doctors and dentists, and there's that. And should you have any questions along the way, I'm gonna be doin' stuff like this, Huck, because you're leaking a little bit out of your mouth there. You're holding my finger, son? Hey, Molly! Your brother's holding my hand. Do you wanna hold my hand?"

And then, in conclusion, "This isn't gonna mean anything to you, but Leo was right. Leo was right."

"I can only hope, sir..."

That Toby has emotional depths seldom seen was made clear in *The West Wing*'s earliest days, when he was summoned by DC police to the scene of a homeless man's death from exposure ("In Excelsis Deo"). Inexplicably moved by the tragedy of this unseen man's death, he undertakes a quiet crusade to learn who he was and restore his dignity, in death. He locates the man's brother, and uses the power of his office to arrange for a military burial, as the man was a veteran.

It all comes to a head in a private scene in the Oval Office, when President Bartlet confronts him over abusing his authority in arranging the funeral. He then restores the President's perspective as he justifies his actions and reveals his heart, in the final exchange:

"Toby, if we start pulling strings like this, you don't think every homeless veteran would come out of the woodwork?"

"I can only hope, sir."

"There's nothing about this that doesn't stink..."

Tasked with getting progressive Supreme Court nominee Roberto Mendoza confirmed by the Senate, Toby finds himself in a backwater police station in Connecticut, bailing the judge out of jail.[23] But Mendoza, wrongly incarcerated, isn't going anywhere: he is enraged by the blatantly racist treatment, has been humiliated in front of his wife and son, and he's determined to push back with all the power of the justice system. And Toby can't let him do that, as satisfying as it might be, because he needs to get him confirmed.

He marshals all his empathy and compassion, determined to connect with the infuriated Mendoza in the shadows of the jail cell:

"If it were me, I'd wanna extract vengeance, and I'd say, 'Let justice be done!' I'd also wanna spend some time in a dark room alone, so that I didn't have to face my wife and my son and have them see my humiliation. Rob, I can't get this done if this is the story. Can't get it done. Nothing about this that doesn't stink. And nothing about it that wouldn't be better if you were a Supreme Court Justice."

"You're my guys..."

A junior staffer in the West Wing has leaked an embarrassing comment of Toby's to a reporter, and it is about to be published – at which point it will be an embarrassment to the President. Toby gets the entire communications staff together in the White House mess to dress them down. But as he's speaking, he locates his sense of community; sitting there in front of him, all around him, he feels connected, and uses that sense of connection to make his point. It's one of the most beautiful Toby moments ever, as we see just how he feels about the people he works with:

"We're a group. We're a team. From the President and Leo on

---

[23] In "Celestial Navigation".

through, we're a team. We win together, we lose together; we celebrate and we mourn together. And defeats are softened and victories sweetened because we did them together. And if you don't like this team, then there's the door...

"I'm not gonna have a witch hunt. I'm not gonna huff and puff. I'm not gonna take anyone's head off. I'm simply gonna say this: you're my guys. And I'm yours. And there's nothing I wouldn't do for you."

...and a bonus Toby moment, for good measure...

"I'm Toby Ziegler. I work at the White House..."

Toby, Josh and Donna have just spent 20 hours in America (in "20 Hours in America"), seeking various modes of transportation and accepting the kindness of strangers as they argue about the Bartlet-Ritchie contest. To amuse themselves, Toby and Josh play a round of toss-the-rock-into-the-trash-can over a wager with the penalty, "Every time you tell someone your name, you have to add, 'I work at the White House'."

Toby is the first to miss, and so Josh is treated to a day of great hilarity as Toby is forced to repeatedly utter, every time he meets someone, "I'm Toby Ziegler... I work at the White House."

They finally land in a hotel restaurant, banished to the bar by Donna for their insensitivities, and Toby finds himself sitting next to a man named Matt Kelley, who tiredly shares his pride in his daughter, whom he has brought to Indiana to look at Notre Dame as a college possibility, while also commiserating that the mutual fund he set up to pay for it isn't performing well. Toby's ears perk up: it's a real-people moment where he gets to have a substantive conversation with an average family man who's willing to air his concerns.

Kelley introduces himself, prompting Toby to do the same. Josh, a little farther down the bar, waves Toby off the bet.

But this time, Toby is very proud to say,

"I'm Toby Ziegler. I work at the White House!"

The Best of Toby Ziegler

"Nobody ever looks like Joe McCarthy. That's how they get in the door in the first place."

~ "The Crackpots and These Women" (S1/E5)

"There is a connection between progress of a society and progress in the Arts. The Age of Pericles was also the Age of Phidias. The Age of Lorenzo de Medici was also the Age of Leonardo Da Vinci. The Age of Elizabeth was the Age of Shakespeare."

~"Gone Quiet" (S3/E6)

"We're running away from ourselves, and I know we can score points that way. I was the principal architect in that campaign strategy, right along with you, Josh. But we're here now. Tomorrow night, we do an immense thing. We have to say what we feel. That government, no matter what its failures are in the past, and in times to come, for that matter, the government can be a place where people come together and where no one gets left behind. *No one...* gets left behind! An instrument of good."

~Toby Ziegler, "He Shall, From Time to Time" (S1/E12)

"In the meantime, a time when the public is rightly concerned about the impact of sex and violence on TV this administration is gonna protect the Muppets, we're gonna protect *Wall Street Week*, we're gonna protect *Live from Lincoln Center*, and by god, we are going to protect Julia Child!"

~"Take Out the Trash Day" (S1/E13)

"There's nothing about this that doesn't stink. If it were me, I'd wanna extract vengeance, and I'd say, 'Let justice be done!' I'd also wanna spend some time in a dark room alone, so that I didn't have to face my wife and my son and have them see my humiliation. Rob, I can't get this done if this is the story. Can't get it done. Nothing about this that doesn't stink. And nothing about it that wouldn't be better if you were a Supreme Court Justice."

~"Celestial Navigation" (S1/E15)

"I think it would be a good idea, as a symbol... to signal that China is serious about their relationship with us, if they stopped running over their citizens with tanks."

~"Six Meetings Before Lunch" (S1/E18)

"I'm disagreeing with you. That doesn't mean I'm not listening to you, or understanding what you're saying. I'm doing all three at the same time."

~"In This White House" (S2/E4)

"Why's the Test Ban Treaty so important? Well! Let me tell you. In 1974 India set off a peaceful nuclear explosion. Indira Ghandi herself said they had no intention of building a bomb, they just wanted to know that they could. Twenty years later, India set off five nuclear explosions. Who gets nervous? Pakistan. When Pakistan get nervous, everyone gets nervous! You know why? 'Cause we're all gonna die."

~"The Lame Duck Congress" (S2/E6)

"I was just thinking about this cartoon I once saw. A bunch of tiny fish are swimming through the leaves of this plant, but then one of the fish realizes it's not a plant, it's the tentacles of a predator. And the fish says, 'with friends like this, who needs anemones?'"

~"The War at Home" (S2/E14)

"You want the benefits of free trade? Food is cheaper. Food is cheaper, clothes are cheaper, steel is cheaper, cars are cheaper, phone service is cheaper. You feel me building a rhythm here? That's 'cause I'm a speechwriter and I know how to make a point. It lowers prices, it raises income. You see what I did with *lowers* and *raises* there? It's called the science of listener attention. We did repetition, we did floating opposites, and now you end with the one that's not like the others; Ready? *Free trade stops wars.* And that's it! Free trade stops wars! And we figure out a way to fix the rest! One world, one peace. I'm sure I've seen that on a sign somewhere."

~ "Somebody's Going to Emergency,
Somebody's Going to Jail" (S2/E16)

"The Commander-In-Chief had just been attacked. He was under a general anesthetic. A fugitive was at large; the manhunt included every federal, state and local law enforcement agency. The Virginia, Maryland, New Jersey, Pennsylvania, and Delaware National Guard was federalized! The KH-10 showed Republican Guard movement in southern Iraq. And 12 hours earlier an F-117 was shot down in the No-Fly, and the Vice President's authority was murky at best! The National Security Advisor and Secretary of State didn't know who they were taking their orders from! I wasn't in the Situation Room that night but I'll bet all the money in my pockets against all the money in your pockets that it was Leo... *who no one elected!* For 90 minutes that night, there was a coup d'etat in this country!"

~"17 People" (S2/E18)

"There's an old saying: 'Those who speak, don't know; and those who know, don't speak.' I don't know if that's true or not, but I know that by and large the press doesn't care who really knows what as long as they've got a quote.

"Last Friday, we had our Week Ahead meeting in the Roosevelt Room. Some of you were there, most of you weren't, but I'm talking to all of you now. Bruno Gianelli and I were leading a discussion about whether or not the President should stop in Kansas on his way back from the West Coast, and I remarked that the Vice President is polling better than the President right now in the Plains states - and that if the President is re-elected, it's gonna be on the Vice President's coattails. That remark made its way to a White House reporter.

"We're a group. We're a team. From the President and Leo on through, we're a team. We win together, we lose together, we celebrate and we mourn together. And defeats are softened and victories sweetened because we did them together. And if you don't like this team - then, there's the door. It's great to be in the know. It's great to have the scoop, to have the skinny, to be able to go to a reporter and say, 'I know something you don't know.' And so the press becomes your constituents and you sell out the team. So, an item will appear in the paper tomorrow, and it'll be embarrassing to me and embarrassing to the President. I'm not gonna have a witch hunt. I'm not gonna huff and puff. I'm not gonna take anyone's head off. I'm simply gonna say this: you're my guys. And I'm yours... and there's nothing I wouldn't do for you."

~"War Crimes" (S3/E5)

"Tawny, you'd need the Budweiser Clydesdales to drag my ass to Picasso and Monet! I'm not the guy you want deciding this! And you're not the guy I want deciding this! And I don't know where you get the idea that taxpayers shouldn't have to pay for anything of which they disapprove? Lots of 'em don't like tanks! Even more don't like Congress!"

~"Gone Quiet" (S3/E6)

"...we love anti-personnel land mines. We love 'em! And we think the government should be in the business of selling them, like the Post Office. In fact, the Post Office is the sales venue we've been considering."

~"The US Poet Laureate" (S3/E16)

"Aha! Time to teach these Stoli-drinking Tchaikovskys a thing or two about free press, American style! You don't ban those who supported your opponent, you make them wallow in their loserdom by covering your victory! You sit them in the front row! You give them a hat! I will save Ludmila Koss, for I am Toby, and in doing so... Why am

I going on like this?"

~"Enemies Foreign and Domestic" (S3/E18)

"...you stink! Last month, you alleged that the Chigorin government bombed several apartment buildings based on an unattributed source. It was refuted; you never retracted! Last week, you had a cover story about President Chigorin's mother-in-law moving closer to the Kremlin. You printed her home address! She had to relocate! You reported the failing grades of the Defense Minister's twelve-year-old son! Does that even count as journalism? Does that do anything but bring ridicule on a defenseless kid?

"We've got people like you here, on cable and on the Internet, and there's no one anywhere on the ideological spectrum that doesn't roll their eyes when their names are spoken out loud! You know, we've always had free press here, we take it for granted... how can you treat it like this? You should give up your space and put another naked woman in there!"

~"Enemies Foreign and Domestic" (S3/E18)

"Do you think he [Gov. Ritchie] ever disagreed with one of his advisors? Do you think – honestly - do you think he's ever said to one of his advisors, 'I've got a different idea?' I don't care if he thinks Luxembourg's an uptown stop on the IRT. And I don't care about the Greco-Roman wrestling matches with the language (not that polished communication skills are an important part of this job)! What I care about is when he was asked if he'd continue the current US policy in China he said, 'First off, I'm going to send them a message - meet an American leader.' I don't know what that means, but everybody cheered."

~"20 Hours in America" (S4/E1)

"I'm Toby Ziegler. I work at the White House."

~"20 Hours in America" (S4/E1)

"I need you to look at a couple of answers on defense readiness. I need concrete examples of waste in Pentagon procurement. We need two more members of the IRC for post spin. I need you to fill out this marriage license and paperwork for a joint checking account, and review this 60-second answer on Rwanda."

~"Debate Camp" (S4/E4)

"See, I lent voice to thought, and that was my mistake."

~"Debate Camp" (S4/E4)

"Of course I wrote a concession! You wanna tempt the wrath of the whatever from high atop the thing?"

~"Election Night" (S4/E6)

"I'm told that on my sunniest of days, I'm not that fun to be around. I wonder what's going to happen when you make my children a part of your life?"

~"Holy Night" (S4/E10)

"Presidential flameout? Makes you feel like you'll never know the love of a real woman."

~"Holy Night" (S4/E10)

"Look, a glass is half full or half... you know, the other thing."

~"Red Haven's on Fire" (S4/E16)

"A meteor fell from the sky the result being two guys are going to get court-marshalled - the only two guys who apparently thought it was strange that North Korea would attack submarines in Connecticut instead of, say, San Diego or Hawaii. And if it had been a real attack? Would they still have been doing point/counterpoint with NORAD? We failed both on a mechanical and human level! So tell me again what

you have faith in."
~"Evidence of Things Not Seen" (S4/E19)

"You've got to ask yourself, if no one on the internet wants a piece of this, just how far from the pack have you strayed?"
~"Evidence of Things Not Seen" (S4/E19)

"I don't know what kind of salad it is! I'm eating a salad, okay? I'm doing it. Do I have to know the names? There's no difference between them! It's a bowl of weeds! Some of them have cheese. This isn't the kind with cheese. Does that answer your question? How many years have you guys been, 'Toby, you eat like a teenager! Toby, that's red meat! That's your second cigar!' Here I am eating a salad – which, by the way, you could cover this thing in barbecue sauce and it would still tastes like the ground - and I'm getting heckled from the gallery, who wanted to come in here to eat his roast beef sandwich with ketchup on a kaiser roll and watch the damn tennis on my TV! That's all I'm saying."
~"Life on Mars" (S4/E20)

"I don't think you've noticed the things I've done to alter the behavior that's troubled you in the past. Giving up what you felt was a bachelor apartment is only the most recent of gestures, which included eating salads."
~"Commencement" (S4/E21)

"My father used to kill people for a living, so, generationally, the Zieglers are making lots of progress."
~"Commencement" (S4/E21)

"I don't know. If, for nine months, you're hearing how this is gonna change your life, and, 'You've never loved anything like this,' and, 'My God, the love' and, 'Nothing's gonna be important anymore.' It just never really felt to me like I was someone who had the capacity for those feelings. Plus, you know, I I like what's important to me. I want it to stay important. I wanna be able to do it well."

~"Twenty-Five" (S4/E22)

"I didn't realize babies come with hats. You guys crack me up. You don't have jobs. You can't walk or speak the language. You don't have a dollar in your pockets, but you got yourselves a hat. So, everything's fine. I don't wanna alarm you or anything, but I'm Dad. And for you, son, for you, this'll be the last time I pass the buck, but I think it should be clear from the get-go that it was Mom who named you Huckleberry. I guess she was feeling like life doesn't present enough challenges to overcome on its own. And, honey, you've got a name now too. Your mom and I named you after an incredibly brave woman, really not all that much older than you. Your name is Molly. Huck and Molly.

"So, what do I do? Well, you're gonna need food and clothes and doctors and dentists, and there's that. And should you have any questions along the way, I'm gonna be doin' stuff like this... Huck, because you're leaking a little bit out of your mouth there. You're holding my finger, son? Hey, Molly. Your brother's holding my hand. Do you wanna hold my hand? This isn't gonna mean anything to you, but Leo was right. Leo was right."

~"Twenty-Five" (S4/E22)

"Yeah, they're great. And if somebody was hurting them, I'd drop napalm on Yellowstone to get them to stop. Letting some prisoners out of jail wouldn't be nothing and I've known my kids for about 45 minutes."

~about his kids, "Twenty-Five" (S4/E22)

"I'm over the moon. This is my over-the-moon face."

~"Jefferson Lives" (S5/E3)

"I'm sure you'd have to say things you haven't meant before. You've read friends' poetry. Had girlfriends."

~"Han" (S5/E4)

"Well, what makes a man seek public office, Josh? What makes a man abjure the comforts of a private life for the Athenian wrestling mat that is the forum politic?"

~"Liftoff" (S6/E4)

"On a scale of one to 10 - 10 being CJ, and one being a chimp throwing feces - where do I rank?"

~"The Hubbert Peak" (S6/E5)

"I hate this issue. It's like walking around town holding a sick chicken."

~"Faith Based Initiative" (S6/E10)

"You're asking me if I knew the military space shuttle was classified? One of the most closely held pieces of information I've encountered in my seven and a half years in the White House, which no one would so much as hint at, much less acknowledge, much less ever actually discuss, which revelation of same caused a governmental security crisis, international consternation and the launching of three separate investigations; you're asking me realized it was classified? Yeah, I had a vague inkling!"

~"Here Today" (S7/E5)

"I believe in an open society. You debate these things in the light of day. That's what's supposed to happen in a democracy."

~"Here Today" (S7/E5)

"Leo McGarry didn't accept his party's nomination to the Vice

Presidency of the United States because he thought it might make your socks roll up and down."

~to Josh, "Running Mates" (S7/E10)

"I read a lot. I've read, really, all the books at this point."

~ "Institutional Memory" (S7/E21)

~TWW~

Legitimate Dude Sightings

Brad Whitford went straight from The West Wing into the starring role of Danny Tripp on Aaron Sorkin's next television series, *Studio 60 on the Sunset Strip*. And from there, he was seen in the following:

- *The Good Guys*, a detective comedy in which he co-starred with Colin Hanks, son of Tom;
- Guest spots on *Monk, Law & Order: LA, The Mentalist,* Rob Lowe's *Parks and Recreation, Law & Order: Special Victims Unit*, a recurring role on *Transparent,* two guest appearances on Allison Janney's *Mom,* and many others;
- He has the role of Commander Joseph Lawrence on the Hulu series *The Hand Maid's Tale*;
- On the big screen, he appeared in *Bottle Shock, The Cabin in the Woods*, Steven Spielberg's *The Post* (alongside Tom Hanks and Meryl Streep), and almost two dozen others;
- One of those others was *Decoding Annie Parker* (2013), in which he appeared with Richard Schiff.

Matt Santos, Child Prodigy

Matt Santos is one amazing guy: Texas congressman, former mayor of Houston, Marine pilot – and, of course, successor to President Josiah Bartlet!

But... that doesn't quite add up, does it?

We learn from Josh, in the sixth season episode "Liftoff", that Santos is only 42 – far too young to be calling it quits! The two argue about this, until Josh comes up with the nine-point plan that nudges Santos into pursuing free-world leadership.

Here's the problem: it's not hard to accept that Santos is 42 as he nears the end of his third term in Congress – at two years per term, that means he was first sent to Washington at 36. JFK was elected to the House when he was only 29, and managed to serve three House terms and advance to the Senate, serving six and a half years there before also turning 42.

But in "The Ticket", the Season Seven opener, we learn from Leo that Santos's six years of Congressional service were preceded by two terms as mayor of Houston – four years each! – meaning he first took office at age 28!

Okay, not unheard of; let's grant all of that, even if it seems somewhat unlikely. But then we have the niggling detail of the 12 years of Marine service, which followed his (presumed) four years of education and training at Annapolis (since it was Annapolis, we know he must have gone into service immediately upon graduation).

This means Santos took up his Marine commission and started flying fighters at 16 – and necessarily was admitted to Annapolis at age 12!

Well, that's all very silly, of course; barring unimaginable circumstances, he started at Annapolis at age 18 and graduated at 22. But that would mean he couldn't have run for anything until he was 34.

Where are the missing years?

We know that Santos is a reservist – a weekend warrior, still a marine but only a part-timer. It would be odd for an Annapolis graduate to go straight into the reserves - but even if he had, the math *still* doesn't work: at age 42, Leo says he served 12 years. We know he didn't begin his service at age 30, he started nearly a decade earlier, at 22. And Leo wasn't adding full-time service to reserve service, because that would be 20 years, not 12. We're forced to conclude that Matt Santos did 12 years of regular active duty, followed by eight years of reserve duty while he was mayoring and Congressing.

And that means he must have been elected as mayor of Houston at age 34 – and for six years of his two terms, *simultaneously serving in Congress!* That boy gets around! Well, when you can fly supersonic fighters, I guess it's not impossible.

But, if so... poor Helen! Not much opportunity for bed-breaking with a husband that busy...

~TWW~

Against all odds, three *West Wing* cast members all grew up in Dayton Ohio: Martin Sheen, Rob Lowe and Allison Janney (Janney's character CJ also grew up there, in WestWingWorld).

According to Fitzgerald & McCormack's *What's Next?*, Rob Lowe once asked Janney where she'd gone to high school, there in Dayton. Her answer: Miami Valley High.

"That was the fancy school," Lowe said, according to *What's Next*; "I was only there once. I was in their gymnasium; they were putting on a production of *A Funning Thing Happened on the Way to the Forum*."

And who was on stage in that play, as Lowe sat there watching? Allison Janney. It was her acting debut, and Lowe was there to see it...

~TWW~

In "We Killed Yamamoto", Donna travels to Bismarck to represent the White House at a conference being held to discuss dropping the word "North" from the name "North Dakota", as a way to boost tourism.

In fact, this is a real thing: in 1947, an attempt was name to drop "North", but it was defeated by the Legislative Assembly; it happened again in 1989, when the Legislature rejected two Senate Concurrent resolutions to rename the state Dakota.

Who said that? (Round 1)

Match the statement with the person who said it.

1. "Nature is to be protected from. Nature, much like a woman, will seduce you with its sights, its scents and its touch. And then it breaks your ankle. Also like a woman."

a. Toby

2. "I'm in some hellish hold world of holding."

b. Bruno Gianelli

3. "We're a group. We're a team, from the President and Leo on through. We're a team. We win together, we lose together. We celebrate and we mourn together. And defeats are softened and victories sweeter because we did them together."

c. CJ

4. "Zippity-do-dah"

d. Mrs. Landingham

5. Ah, sarcasm – the grumpy man's wit."

e. Oliver Babish

6. "You're wrong! Just stand there in your wrongness and be wrong!"

f. Josh

7. "This country is an idea, and one that's lit the world for two centuries!"

g. Jed Bartlet

8. "I'm gonna crush him, I'm gonna make him cry, and then I'm gonna tell his momma about it!"

h. Sam

Who Said That? (Round 1) Answers

1. e
2. f
3. a
4. b
5. d
6. g
7. h
8. c

~TWW~

In "Take This Sabbath Day", Karl Malden plays a priest, and takes a small bible out of his pocket. It is the same bible he used when performing in *On the Waterfront* (1954).

~TWW~

Real-world newspeople and writers mentioned on The West Wing:

- Walter Cronkite ("18th and Potomac")
- Bob Woodward ("The War at Home")
- Bill Maher ("17 People")
- Ann Coulter ("17 People", "20 Hours in America")

~TWW~

The 17 people in "17 People" are Abbey, Liz, Ellie, Zoey; the President's brother Jonathan; six doctors who examined him at the onset of the MS; Vice President John Hoyes; Admiral Fitzwallace; Leo; Dr. David Lee, the anesthesiologist at GW; Toby; and President Bartlet.

The Top 10 Sam Moments

Like his boss, Leo shines particularly bright in several key scenes. There are more (as they are with all the characters), but this is a start:

"This country is an idea, and one that's lit the world
for two centuries!"

It's Big Block of Cheese Day, and Sam winds up helping Donna with a unique problem.[24] He's also in charge of reviewing pardon applications, and Donna has an old college friend who is looking for exactly that: a Presidential pardon for her deceased grandfather, who had been a State Department official accused of being a Soviet agent.

Presented with evidence from Nancy McNally that the man was indeed an agent, Sam is enraged, and when Donna finds him, he is so filled with emotion that can hardly hold it together. In this moment, all of Sam's passion for his country and the values he is pledged to serve comes surging out as Donna watches:

"Treason against that idea is not just a crime against the living! This ground holds the graves of people who died for it, who gave what Lincoln called the last full measure of devotion. Of fidelity. You understand the last full measure of devotion to... Treason against them is..." And he is so overwhelmed that he has to pause and collect himself.

His rage is so strong that he comes perilously close to unleashing it on Donna's friend; but he recovers his compassion and offers a benign excuse to put her off, sparing her the truth about her grandfather. We see two admirable sides, then, of Sam; the sheer force of his love of country, alongside his deep kindness.

"Sir, we expect the President to face the world in his own way,

---

[24] In "Somebody's Going to Emergency, Somebody's Going to Jail".

for his own time."

As the senior staff and an assortment of supporting personnel help prep President Bartlet for his debate with Gov. Ritchie,[25] Sam (who does a great Bartlet imitation) has a brief private conversation with his boss, who in a rare unguarded moment shares some insecurity he's feeling, after having a past mistake brought back to mind:

"I don't mind blowing the knucklehead stuff like Rooker... Rooker's not knucklehead, but if I'm making mistakes there, how do I know I'm not doing it when it comes to matters like death and destruction?"

The question is rhetorical, but Sam nonetheless offers reassurance. It's a strong moment, in which Sam not only embeds his loyalty in his supporting answer, but gives Bartlet permission to be human.

"When I write something, I sign my name!"

Sam's embarrassment over having been trounced on live air by Ainsley Hayes on *Capital Beat* bubbles over when Leo hires her for the White House Counsel's office, and Lionel Tribbey sends her to fix a potential issue with mistaken Congressional testimony given by two arrogant staffers.[26] The two are not at all welcoming of Ainsley's advice, and contemptuous of her even for approaching them.

When a bout of rudeness from Sam sends Ainsley, disheartened, back to her desk in the Steam Pipe Trunk Distribution Venue, she is greeted by a vase filled with dead flowers and a card bearing the word BITCH. Sam walks up behind her, sees the card – and in a heartbeat, is a man transformed.

He realizes what has happened, and in a fury descends on the two staffers, grabbing a large sheet of paper and writing YOU'RE FIRED! SAM SEABORN.

As unwelcoming as he himself had been, it takes only the look in the mirror that the staffers' disrespect offers for him to spring to her defense, all too aware of his own behavior. From that moment forward,

---

[25] In "Debate Camp".

[26] In "And It's Surely to Their Credit."

he treats Ainsley as part of the team.

"Well, we play with live ammo around here!"

Ainsley offers Sam more than an opportunity to practice what he preaches. When he assigns her to summarize a position recommendation he intends to present to the President on white collar fraud policy, she reverses his position, and he finds himself in a lengthy argument with her, telling why he's right as she explains why he's wrong (in "The Lame Duck Congress").

When he's caught in a clichéd assumption, he pauses to hear her, and with fresh ears he absorbs her argument – and is persuaded. He actually *does* reverse his position, not too proud to take up a new point of view when presented with a compelling argument. Leo approves it.

Ainsley is mortified. "I was just talking, Sam, I was just talking to you! Because I said in here... the President in there..." She can't believe that simply offering Sam a different point of view would result in an administration policy change. Sam quips, "It's a short day, Ainsley, and a big country. We've gotta move fast!"

That marvelous scene showcases both Sam's fitness for public service as a person open to new information and reasoned argument, and Ainsley's awe over the actual nuts and bolts of public policy.

"We came out of the cave, looked over the hill and saw fire!"

The *Galileo* probe has gone quiet, and Sam is helping the President with alternate themes for the virtual classroom event planned around it.[27] He and CJ accompany the President to a concert at the Kennedy Center – where he runs into Mallory.

He has a bumpy history with her, and is skittish until she raises the question of why we should spend so much money sending robots to crash on Mars when we could be putting the money into public education. His response is one of *The West Wing*'s greatest speeches:

"There are a lot of hungry people in the world, Mal, and none of

---

[27] In "Galileo".

them are hungry because we went to the moon. None of them are colder, and certainly none of them are dumber 'cause we went to the moon!

"The history of man is hung on the timeline of exploration, and this is what's next!"

Isn't it great how he worked 'What's next?' into his speech?

> *"Instead of buying these ships – don't buy these ships.*
> *Buy other ships. Better ships!"*

In the pre-Bartlet Administration, flashbacked in an anesthesia-induced haze during Josh's emergency surgery for bullet removal,[28] Sam sits in a conference room with the Gage Whitney team as they explain to Kensington Oil about the tankers they are buying on their behalf.

Sam has spent some time thinking about the deal – big bargains negotiated in the purchase of outdated, not-so-great oil tankers. A principle architect of the deal, he has a change of heart.

"Don't buy these ships," he tells their clients, "buy better ships!"

He makes his appeal on moral grounds: ships this iffy, carrying hundreds of thousands of barrels of oil, present a serious hazard to the environment. Buying them to save money – buying them *at all* – is irresponsible, he believes.

Before Mr. Gage can fire him, Josh comes along and smiles him out of the room and onto the Bartlet for America campaign. But wasn't it great, seeing him stand up for the right thing?

> *"I think it will, too!"*

An attack ad targeting Jed Bartlet has been anonymously delivered to the Bartlet campaign. The staff review it, and Bruno Gianelli insists it be stuck in a drawer with no response.

Sam idealistically suggests that he meet with his old friend Kevin Kahn, who works for the other side. He sees no harm in getting the

---

[28] In "In the Shadow of Two Gunmen, Pt. II".

poisonous thing out of their office altogether and disavowing it utterly. Kahn accepts the video, feigning gratitude for Sam's forthrightness (in "The Black Vera Wang").

It's a setup. Kahn is playing on his old friend's nobility, allowing himself to be tricked into serving up the video as scathing free advertising for Ritchie – as retribution for President Bartlet's "open mic" incident, which was insulting to Ritchie.

Sam confronts him that night in the rainy street, and their confrontation is fierce. Sam's spirit of honesty and fair play have been exploited, and now his righteousness is roaring to the fore. It's on. He won't be played twice.

"Is it going to happen again?" Kahn taunts, "I think it will!"

"I think it will, too!"

"I came this close to voting for him!"

In the wake of President Bartlet's re-election victory, Sam and the other senior staffers are talking about Sam's new status as a Congressional candidate,[29] and he shares a story of a State Assembly race in Manhattan he'd helped with. He remembered a "right-wing nutbar" fringe candidate who kept showing up at campaign events waving signs about eliminating the income tax. Sam remembered seeking out the guy's manager, insisting that the guy didn't have a chance.

The candidate's position: "This is what I believe. And no candidate gets to run in my district without speaking to my issues!"

Sam says he came close to voting for the guy; he shared Sam's own conviction that the Democratic process itself means far more than any one issue ever could.

"In a country born of a will to be free, what could be more fundamental than this?"

President Bartlet's nominee for the Supreme Court, Peyton Cabot

---

29 In "Process Stories".

Harrison III, doesn't believe the Constitution support the right to privacy. Sam discovers this in reading through his old papers, and brings it to the attention of Toby and the President, who bring Harrison in for a chat. It's clear from his comments that Sam is right about him; they will need to find a new nominee.

Sam summarizes the reasons why, in one of his most eloquent moments:

"It's about the next 20 years. Twenties and Thirties, it was the role of government. Fifties and Sixties, it was civil rights. The next two decades, it's gonna be privacy: I'm talking about the Internet; I'm talking about cellphones; I'm talking about health records, and who's gay and who's not. And moreover, in a country born on a will to be free, what could be more fundamental than this?"

"One of us is getting on a plane tonight..."

Josh has managed the Santos campaign to victory, and has lured Sam into forsaking Los Angeles to join the new administration as his deputy chief of staff. Sam arrives in LA, only to find that Josh is a burned-out mess; he looks like hell and is snapping at people.

Sam realizes Josh is nearing his breaking point, and presents an ultimatum that is a thinly-disguised act of brotherly love: Josh can get out of town for a week, during which he will mind the store; or he'll head back home and that will bet that. It's both a demonstration of the new professional dynamic that will be essential to their administration and a beautiful expression of friendship.

This message gets through, and Josh gets on a plane – with Donna at his side.

~TWW~

The newspaper picturing Toby and President Bartlet in the Oval Office on its front page used in "Celestial Navigation" is later seen framed on the wall of Toby's office in "Holy Night".

The Best of Sam Seaborn

"Mallory, education is the silver bullet! Education *is everything!* We don't need little changes, we need gigantic, monumental changes! Schools should be palaces! The competition for the best teachers should be fierce! They should be making six-figure salaries! School should be incredibly expensive for government and absolutely free of charge to its citizens, just like national defense. That's my position. I just haven't figured out how to do it yet."

~"Six Meetings Before Lunch" (S1/E18)

"...she broke your heart! You know the way women can do, where they take your heart and they throw it on the floor and then they stomp on it with their big high heels..."

~"Mandatory Minimums" (S1/E20)

"Well over three and a half centuries ago, strengthened by faith and bound by a common desire for liberty, a small band of pilgrims sought out a place in the New World where they could worship according to their own beliefs. And solve crimes."

~"Shibboleth" (S2/E8)

"'Good morning. Eleven months ago, a 1,200-pound spacecraft blasted off from Cape Canaveral, Florida. Eighteen hours ago-' Is it eighteen hours ago? We're on the air at noon eastern. '-Eighteen hours ago, it landed on the planet Mars. You, me, and 60,000 of your fellow students across the country, along with astroscientists and engineers from the Jet Propulsion Lab in Southern California, NASA Houston, and right here at the White House, are going to be the first to see what it sees, and to chronicle an extraordinary voyage of an unmanned ship called *Galileo V*.'"

~"Galileo" (S2/E9)

"[We really need to go to Mars] 'Cause it's next! 'Cause we came out of the cave, and we looked over the hill, and we saw fire! And we crossed the ocean, and we pioneered the West, and we took to the sky! The history of man is hung on the timeline of exploration, and this is what's next!"

~"Galileo" (S2/E9)

"Okay. The difference between a good speech and a great speech is the energy with which the audience comes to their feet at the end. Is it polite? Is it a chore? Are they standing up because their boss is standing up? No, we want it to come from their socks!"

~"The Drop-In" (S2/E12)

"This country is an idea, and one that's lit the world for two centuries! And treason against that idea is not just a crime against the living! This ground holds the graves of people who died for it, who gave what Lincoln called the last full measure of devotion!"

~"Somebody's Going to Emergency, Somebody's Going to Jail"
(S2/E16)

"I left Gage Whitney making $400,000 a year, which means I paid 27 times the national average in income tax. I paid my fair share, and the fair share of 26 other people. And I'm happy to, 'cause that's the only way it's gonna work, and it's in my best interest that everybody be able to go to schools and drive on roads. But I don't get 27 votes on Election Day. The fire department doesn't come to my house 27 faster and the water doesn't come out of my faucet 27 times hotter. The top one percent of wage earners in this country pay for 22 percent of this country. Let's not call them names while they're doing it, is all I'm saying."

~"The Fall's Gonna Kill You" (S2/E20)

"Over the past half-century, we've split the atom, we've spliced the gene, and we've roamed Tranquility Base. We've reached for the stars, and never have we been closer to having them in our grasp. New science, new technology is making the difference between life and death, and so we need a national commitment equal to this unparalleled moment of possibility. And so, I announce to you tonight, that I will bring the full resources of the federal government and the full reach of my office to this fundamental goal: we will cure cancer by the end of this decade."

~"100,000 Airplanes" (S3/E11)

"Yeah, except, that's *not* all you know, because you're bright and you're curious and you worked hard, and you got into Smith and you got your law degree where? Cambridge, Massachusetts. You lose, I win! 'Twas ever thus."

~"The US Poet Laureate" (S3/E16)

"It's hard not to like a guy who doesn't know 'frumpy' but knows 'onomatopoeia'."

~"Enemies Foreign and Domestic" (S3/E18)

"I worked in a State Assembly race in Manhattan in a district where Democrats outnumbered Republicans 16 to 1. But everywhere we went, there'd be one lone poster of a right-wing nutbar who wanted to eliminate the income tax. And he was holding up signs and canvassing everywhere and bugging the local reporters until we had to comment on it. So I introduced myself to his campaign manager, and I said, 'What are you doing? Your candidate doesn't have a chance and neither do your issues.' He said, 'This is what I believe. And no candidate gets to run in my district without speaking to my issue.' I came this close to voting for him."

~Sam, "Process Stories" (S4/E7)

Critiquing the Bartlet Presidency: Thumbs Down!

The Bartlet Presidency got a good review above. Most fans of the show would agree with what's said about his performance and accomplishments in office.

But fair is fair – not everyone feels that way. Some critics have rated his tenure as "mediocre". One such critic is Ian Millhiser, who wrote a detailed analysis in 2012 for *ThinkProgress*.

"The Bartlet Administration had few bold ideas," Millhiser wrote. "What was the Bartlet plan to ensure universal access to health care? Or the Bartlet plan to combat global warming? What did President Bartlet do to close the education gap between poor and rich children? Or to ensure that every child who does succeed in high school will be able to pay for college?"

Millhiser's assessment of Bartlet's progressive efforts is that they amounted to appeasement to his peers and lip service to the general public:

"Ultimately," he wrote, "his presidency advances a very small kind of liberalism that appeals mostly to people who've never worried if they could pay their medical bills or if their children can afford college."

Comparing Bartlet to Bush II, he wrote that the latter accomplished more, in the end: Bartlet expanded Medicare to include mammograms and cancer clinical trials; Bush signed off on prescription drugs for seniors. Bush gracefully surrendered on efforts to privatize social security; Bartlet accommodated Congressional privatizers.

Bartlet, Millhiser wrote, "consistently favored symbolic cultural victories over real opportunities to make life better for American families."

No path to universal healthcare was ever presented by the Bartlet Administration; no concrete plan to address global warming was ever put forth. The Bartlet White House's very vocal commitment to education, Millhiser points out, was ultimately hollow: in the end, he signed off on support for school vouchers.

Millhiser further argues that the "3.8 million new jobs" Bartlet claims in his cathedral showdown with the Lord sounds like more than it is; it amounts to a little over 90,000 new jobs for each month of his presidency, which is just enough to keep up with population growth. He further argues that the victory of the Mendoza appointment to the Supreme Court was severely offset by the later appointment of Christopher Mulready.

"Ultimately, the Bartlet Administration was a failed opportunity because President Bartlet never once sought out these kinds of battles," Millhiser wrote. "Protecting choice or welcoming gays into the military (something the Bartlet Administration supported but never accomplished) are important prongs of the progressive agenda, but a liberalism that's uninterested in income inequality or ensuring that no American ever dies because they cannot afford to treat a curable disease is both a recipe for electoral defeat and a tragedy of moral neglect."

Agree? Or no?

~TWW~

Legitimate Dude Sightings

Richard Schiff has stayed busy since The West Wing, logging plenty of time on screen at home and in theaters:

- He appeared in David Gerrold's *Martian Child*, along with Amanda Peet (from *Studio 60*);
- He shared the screen with Brad Whitford in *Decoding Annie Parker*;
- He played Dr. Emil Hamilton in *Man of Steel* (2013);
- He was in *Take Me to the River, The Frozen Ground, Geostorm, Clemency*, and more than a dozen other films, including
- *Black Panther: Wakanda Forever* (as the US Secretary of State);
- On TV, he starred on *The Good Doctor* as Aaron Glassman (121 episodes);
- He did guest spots on *Monk*, Allison Janney's *Mom, Burn Notice, The Sarah Conner Chronicles, NCIS, Bones, Key & Peele, Once Upon a Time*, and many others.

The Best of Charlie Young

"Sir, I need you to dig in now: it wasn't a nightmare; you really are the President."

~Charlie, "Celestial Navigation" (S1/E15)

"Hey, look! It says here that a hundred years ago, a black guy couldn't show up to a club opening with a white girl for fear he'd be killed."

~Charlie, "The White House Pro Am" (S1/E17)

"My philosophy of self-defense has a lot to do with running as fast as I possibly can."

~Charlie, "Bad Moon Rising" (S2/E19)

"I'll stay with my team. People should stop trying to get me not to do that."

~"On the Day Before" (s3/E4)

"I know how much you like to think of yourself as a man of the people, Roman references and all - but you're the only person who can launch our nuclear weapons. You travel in a fully secured perimeter. You rescue submarines. Maybe it's time that an aide delivers a piece of paper?"

~Charlie, "Gone Quiet" (S3/E6)

"You're a smart, savvy woman who could easily consider world domination for a next career move."

~Charlie, to CJ, "Election Day, Pt. I" (S7/E16)

Home Sweet Home!

The West Wing is, of course, a workplace drama, not a domestic one, and so almost all the action takes place in the office. Many TV shows of the past, however, managed to do a great job of presenting both office and home – The *Dick Van Dyke Show* and *Mary Tyler Moore Show* each did a great job of this.

In the modern era – not so much. We hardly ever see where detectives, forensic investigators or doctors go when the day is done.

But while *The West Wing* is much more the former than the latter (unless you count the White House residence, where we have dozens and dozens of domestic scenes), we do get the occasional glimpse of our characters' inner sanctums. Here's a rundown:

Josh is unquestionably the domestic king. We first see his place from the outside, not long after he's been shot, as he sits on the stoop at night with his peers in his oversize jammies, having an ordnance-violating beer ("The Midterms"). We see the inside of it in flashback in "Noël", as he surfaces the memory of putting his hand through a window. Once he starts his relationship with Amy, we seem to be in a different apartment (understandable; the old one would probably have some bad memories), and observe his morning routine, which involved reusing old coffee grounds. We also see the place decked out in Tahitian décor for a stay-home with Amy.

We see Amy's place not long after in "We Killed Yamamoto", when a lazy Sunday the two are enjoying gets interrupted for a back-in-the-office meeting that puts them at odds on a reauthorization bill, as Van Morrison croons, and again the next episode ("Posse Comitatus"), as their fight over the reauthorization bill is interrupted by a phone call informing that Simon Donovan was shot and killed.

Finally, years later, we're back to Josh's apartment, when Donna appears at his door - and isn't there to talk ("Transition").

If we're not counting the White House residence as Jed and Abbey Bartlet's home-sweet-home, that's okay, because we get to see their *actual* home – their New Hampshire farm, Awasiwi Odinak ("Far from the things of man") in "Manchester, Pts. I and II" (we even get to visit the barn, where the garter snakes are harmless). And we return later – or CJ does, anyway – on the occasion of Zoey's post-kidnapping interview with the dictator-tormenting Diane Mathers ("Separation of Powers").

Then there's Leo. We see the home he shares with wife Jenny twice before that status shifts; once in the pilot episode, where he does a crossword puzzle while eating breakfast, and again on the night of their anniversary – which he forgets ("Five Votes Down").

We know Leo moved into a hotel, because he told Mallory he wanted her mom to have the house – and we see that hotel after his surgery, where a nurse looks after him.

Toby – well, lots going on there. We know that after he and Andy divorced, he moved into what he thinks she felt was a "bachelor apartment," which he was happy to jettison in order to provide her with her dream house, Jefferson Wyler's place, if she will just remarry him. Alas, Toby is sad, and not warm, and she declines ("Commencement"). She gets another house, which Toby visits to help with young Huck and Molly's trick-or-treating ("Welcome to Wherever You Are").

We see Toby in his apartment, talking to Josh (who's out on the campaign trail) on the phone – not because we need to see this "bachelor apartment", but because he no longer has an office (in "Two Weeks Out"). But we only see Toby at his desk, talking on the phone. We don't really see the place until Josh actually drops by, in "Undecideds". And finally, CJ visits Toby at home as she bounces around one evening, trying to decide what to do with her life – their final scene together[30] (in "Institutional Memory").

The thing is – the apartment CJ visits *is not the same apartment Josh visits.*

Let's remember, Toby is on his way to prison. He has nothing to do but cook chicken, review the Constitution and read, really, all the books. When Josh visits him, it's still a horse race between Santos and Vinick; when CJ visits, transition is almost complete, so it's a few months in time between the two visits. But we're forced to ask – why

---

[30] And Richard Schiff's series wrap.

in the world, in that brief period, did Toby feel the need to move into a new place?

Sam. Sam, Sam, Sam. You'd think with his casual barroom dalliances and much more fraught attempts at substantive relationships – particularly that bumpy one with the boss's daughter – that'd we'd have seen quite a lot of Sam's place (though we can take him at his word that he's never seen Cathy naked).

But no. We see Sam's place only once, in "20 Hours in America", where he's getting much-needed sleep after a long stretch without any, and Josh calls from Possum Gulch, Indiana to rouse him and inform him that he's going to have to go back in and staff the President.

Pre-Bartlet Administration, CJ had a beautiful place in Los Angeles, high above the city, complete with a swimming pool that she fell in. We briefly glimpsed the inside when we saw her awakened by a phone call from her boss Isabel ("In the Shadow of Two Gunmen, Pt. II").

We see CJ's Washington place a couple of times. The first is immediately after her ascension to Chief of Staff, when she is visited at 5:26am by military personnel who brief her on which nearby field to stand in, should there be a nuclear attack ("Liftoff"). A less apocalyptic moment is served up when we see her and Danny, with him she has now gone coital, getting ready for work together ("Institutional Memory").

There's a brief glimpse of Donna's second-floor apartment in "Inauguration: Over There", when Josh and Toby and Danny and Charlie and Will all accost one of her windows with snowballs, to draw her outdoors so that Josh can scold her for taking the rap for Jack Reese, who leaked something he shouldn't have to the press. We don't go inside, however.

Oddly, we see more of the Santos domicile than we do the Bartlet farm – but this, of course, is due to the whole presidential campaign story arc, where we watch Matt Santos go from retiring congressman to President Bartlet's successor, and get an inside look at how it all affects his family life.

The first appearance happens when Josh flies out to Houston to pitch his nine-point plan ("Impact Winter"). After he leaves, we listen in as Santos tells his wife Helen about Josh's visit ("Faith Based Initiative"). We return after Santos lands the Democratic nomination and his family adapts to the Secret Service fortification of their home ("Running Mates").

We get just a brief glimpse of Arnold Vinick's home in Washington just after the election, when he goes outside in the morning to pick up the paper; we follow him back into his stately townhouse, which reflects the Republican lifestyle he deserves ("The Last Hurrah").

Finally, we get a very quick flurry of home-behind-the-scenes in the opening of "Requiem", the episode where we say goodbye to Leo, as those about to attend his funeral are all getting dressed. We see, in succession, President Bartlet, CJ, Josh, Toby, and Donna, each staring somberly into their bedroom mirrors as they prepare to leave for the service.

That leaves Charlie and Will, whose digs we never saw. But wouldn't they have been interesting?

~TWW~

In "20 Hours in LA", Donna is star-struck poolside at Ted Marcus's fundraiser and mentions spotting Matthew Perry in the crowd. The actual Matthew Perry, of course, appeared later in three episodes as Associate White House Counsel Joe Quincy.

A similar collision of actor on screen with mention of their real-world self occurred on Studio 60 on the Sunset Strip, where Christine Lahti guest-starred as journalist Martha O'Dell – only to have "Christine Lahti" invoked several episodes later when someone says to Allison Janney, appearing as herself, "Loved you on *Chicago Hope!*"

Alma Mater

The Bartlet White House is filled with very, very smart people. It's impossible to watch 10 minutes of any episode without this being utterly clear.

It starts at the top, of course; President Jed Bartlet is a supremely intelligent, well-educated and well-read man, with world-class credentials. And, as most very wise people do, he surrounded himself with more intelligent people.

Here are their credentials.

President Bartlet
University of Notre Dame
BA, American Studies (minor in Theology)
London School of Economics
MS, PhD
Dartmouth University
Honorary Doctorate, Humane Letters

Leo McGarry
Leo attended the University of Michigan, and he has a law degree:
"Everybody in the room is a lawyer" (Sam)
"Say the word, we'll take a leave of absence and join your legal
team" (Leo, to Josh) –"And It's Surely to Their

Credit"

Josh Lyman

Harvard University (undergrad)
Yale University (law degree)

CJ Cregg

National Merit Scholar
Williams College (undergrad)
University of California at Berkeley
    MS, Political Science

Toby Ziegler

Ditto Leo: though no school is specified, Leo has a law degree:
    "Everybody in the room is a lawyer" (Sam)
    "Say the word, we'll take a leave of absence and join your legal
        team" (Leo, to Josh), in "And It's Surely
        to Their Credit"

Sam Seaborn

Duke University (undergrad)
Princeton University (law degree)

Will Bailey

Carnegie Mellon University
    (conjecture; he is wearing a Carnegie Mellon sweatshirt
    while jogging at Camp David in "NSF Thurmont")
University of Cambridge
    (on a Marshall scholarship; he served as President

of the Cambridge Union Society)

Ainsley Hayes
Smith College (undergrad)
Harvard Law School (law degree)

Mandy Hampton
BA, Art History
MS, Communications
PhD, Political Science

Charlie Young
Theodore Roosevelt High School (Washington, DC)
Georgetown University (law degree)

Zoey Bartlet
Georgetown University

Kennedys!

We noted above that there's great overlap, actor-wise, between *The West Wing* and the Kennedy historical drama *Thirteen Days*. And we've noted that JFK is, himself, acknowledged in WestWingWorld, in many episodes – "Tomorrow", in particular.

We also noted that Martin Sheen had played Bobby Kennedy. Turns out he has also played Bobby's older brother John in the 1983 TV mini-series *Kennedy*.

But it also turns out he isn't the only *West Wing* actor to play JFK. Here are the others:

- Rob Lowe (Sam Seaborn), in Killing Kennedy (2013);
- Tim Matheson (Vice President John Hoynes), concurrent with this *West Wing* tenure, in *Jacqueline Bouvier Kennedy Onassis* (2000);
- William Devane (Secretary of State Lewis Berryhill), with Martin Sheen (as Bobby) in *The Missiles of October* (1974);
- Daniel Hugh Kelly (Tech lobbyist James Cook in "Talking Points"), in *Jackie, Ethel & Joan: The Women of Camelot* (2001);

Another relevant entry – an actor who isn't from WestWingWorld but is part of the Sorkinverse: Steven Weber, who played network president Jack Rudolph in Studio 60 on the Sunset Strip. He played JFK in The Kennedys of Massachusetts (1990).

And we should mention that the most famous John Kennedy movie of all – Oliver Stone's *JFK* (1991) – is narrated by (wait for it!) Martin Sheen...

~TWW~

The real Josiah Bartlett, signatory to the Declaration of Independence and Articles of Confederation – Jed Bartlet's great-grandfather's great-grandfather – spelled his last name with three t's, not two.

Guest Stars

Match the actor to their role on *The West Wing*.

1. Ed Begley, Jr.
2. Tom Skerritt
3. Oliver Platt
4. Christopher Lloyd
5. Glenn Close
6. Laura Dern
7. Janeane Garofolo
8. Mason Adams
9. Nick Searcy
10. John Larouquette Shallick
11. Mel Harris
12. Matthew Perry
13. Carl Lumbly

a. Supreme Court Justice Joseph Crouch

b. SCOTUS nominee Roberto Mendoza

c. Asst. AG nominee Jeff Breckenridge

d. Film mogul Ted Marcus

e. Lord John Marbury

f. White House Council Lionel Tribbey

g. Joey Lucas

h. White House Council Oliver Babish

i. Associate WH Council Joe Quincy

j. Congressman Henry

k. Senator Seth Gillette

l. Asst. Secretary of State Albie Duncan

m. Poet-Laureate Tabitha Fortis

14. Brian Dennehy   n. Chief Justice Evelyn Baker Lang

15. Edward James Olmos   o. Cathy the wholesome farmgirl

16. Corbin Bernsen   p. Marco Arlens

17. Hal Holbrook   q. Sen. George Montgomery

18. Roger Rees   r. Congressman Nate Singer

19. Amy Adams   s. Frank Hollis

20. Matthew Modine   t. Sen. Ricky Rafferty

21. Bob Balaban   u. Sen. Rafe Framhagen

22. Marlee Matlin   v. Louise (Lou) Thornton

23. Robert Foxworth   w. Sen. Chris Carrick

24. Xander Berkeley   x. Prof. Lawrence Lessig

GUEST STARS ANSWERS

1. k
2. w
3. h
4. x
5. n
6. m
7. v
8. a
9. r
10. f
11. t
12. i
13. c
14. u
15. b
16. j
17. l
18. e
19. o
20. p
21. d
22. g
23. q
24. s

~TWW~

In the New Hampshire Bartlet for America campaign headquarters, seen in "In the Shadow of Two Gunmen, Pt. II", the words "It's the Economy, Stupid" – Bill Clinton's 1992 campaign theme – are seen written on a white board.

The Best of Mrs. Landingham

"The President has nothing but free time, Toby. Right now he's in the residence eating Cheerios and enjoying Regis and Kathie Lee. Should I get him for you?"

~"Post Hoc, Ergo Propter Hoc" (s1/E2)

"I miss my boys... Twins. Andrew and Simon. I tried not, you know, I dressed them differently, but they still did everything together. They went off to medical school together, and then they finished their second year at the same time, and of course their lottery number came up at the same time... they wanted to go where people needed doctors. Their father and I begged them, but you can't tell kids anything. So they joined up as medics and four months later they were pinned down during a fight in DaNang and were killed by enemy fire. That was Christmas Eve 1970. You know, they were so young, Charlie, they were your age. It's hard when that happens so far away, you know because, with the noises and the shooting, they had to be so scared. It's hard not to think that right then they needed their mother... Anyway, I miss my boys."

~"In Excelsis Deo" (S1/E10)

"Caesar's wife must be above reproach!"

~"18th and Potomac" (s2/E21)

"Look at you. You're a boy king! You're a foot smarter than the smartest kid in the class. You're blessed with inspiration, you must know this by now. You must have sensed it."

~Young Mrs. Landingham, "Two Cathedrals" (S2/E22)

"You know, if you don't want to run again, I respect that. But if you don't run 'cause you think it's gonna be too hard or you think you're

gonna lose - well, God, Jed, I don't even want to know you."
~"Two Cathedrals" (S2/E22)

"I'm happy to get him myself, as they do in the civilized world."
~"Bartlet for America" (S3/E9)

~TWW~

A decade after *The West Wing* ended, latter-day cast member Josh Malina (Will Bailey) teamed up with wingnut superfan Hrishikesh Hirway on their podcast The West Wing Weekly, a love letter to the show that cranked out four years' worth of episodes.

The premise of the show was simple – to revisit each episode of the series, commenting on them, often with cast members and crew members as guests. Dulé Hill was the first, followed by Janel Moloney, Richard Schiff, Melissa Fitzgerald, Rob Lowe, Allison Janney, Brad Whitford, Kristin Chenowith, Alan Alda, and Martin Sheen.

Frequent guests Marlee Matlin, Emily Proctor, Kathleen York, Tim Matheson, Oliver Platt, Gary Cole, Michael O'Neill and Clark Gregg, among many others, also dropped in. Guest stars Penn & Teller, Mark Harmon, Jason Isaacs and others also joined in.

Crew members and production personnel who guested on the podcast included Eli Attie, Christopher Misiano, Debora Cahn, Lawrence O'Donnell, and many others – including Aaron Sorkin and Tommy Schlamme.

And real-world politicians, including Pete Buttigieg, Antony Blinken, Justin Trudeau, Tom Daschle and others dropped by, as well as political consultant David Axelrod, former White House Communications Director Donald Baer, and other political pros.

The series wrapped up in 2019, and can still be heard at www. thewestwingweekly.com.

"I'm a terrible actor!"

Every TV cast has its merry pranksters. On the original *Star Trek*, it was Captain Kirk himself, William Shatner, who enjoyed stealing Leonard Nimoy's bicycle and hiding it in the soundstage rafters, or stashing his Great Dane Butler in other actors' trailers.

On *The West Wing* set, it was Josh Malina, whose pranks leaned mercilessly into the cruel-and-unusual – unleashing the retribution of another merry prankster.

In *What's Next*, Fitzgerald and McCormack describe Malina as "the Meanest Man in the World", and devote an entire chapter to revelations of his shameless malfeasance. They describe a man without restraint, without boundaries – a prankster so in love with the craft that the idea of "limits" was a bridge too far.

"The thing is, Malina has no sense of proportional response," Brad Whitford is reported as saying. "If I used a hand buzzer on him, he would, you know, pick up my daughter from school and not tell me."

Amid the reports in *What's Next*: how Malina put an open bag of flour on top of Alex Graves' office door so it would fall on him when he walked in; how he stole Graves' iPod and erased all 8,000 songs, then reset the device to Mandarin; how he hid an onion in Allison Janney's trailer, so it would rot there.

He hazed a new director by pilfering props and computers, and using the director's keys (borrowed from a teamster), stashed it all in the director's trunk – then called the police and reported it all stolen. He got his own father to call another cast member, pretending to be an IRS agent instigating an audit; and he supplemented sweet Post-It notes left for Whitford by his assistant with sweet Post-Its of his own: "You've peaked!" "You're losing your hair!" "The reward is death!"

Well, according to Fitzgerald and McCormack, when Malina crossed Whitford, he awakened a sleeping giant.

Brad Whitford had the opportunity to write a couple of the later episodes – "Faith Based Initiative" and "Internal Displacement" – and on the latter, he had had enough of Malina's pranks to have decided it was on. So he put the lines, "I can't act! I'm a terrible actor!" in Will Bailey's mouth, as part of the story.

"Malina would have to say, multiple times, 'I'm a terrible actor' on national television," according to *What's Next*.

As well-played as that counter-prank was, Whitford had the ingenuity to keep milking it. F&M go on to report that in 2023, he talked a sound engineer into playing the audio of that episode clip over the speakers before the curtain came up on a live performance of *Leopoldstadt* on Broadway, in which Malina was playing. Better still, he later had the entire clip played on the super-huge Jumbotron screen at Citi Field during a Mets game – as Malina looked on in the crowd.

He was a good sport about it, of course (as he had to be, to keep on living): *What's Next* reports that when *TWW* cast members picketed in solidarity with the Writers Guild of America and Screen Actors Guild, Malina's picket sign read, "I CAN'T ACT. I'M A TERRIBLE ACTOR. PAY ME."

~TWW~

Besides past presidents, famous politicians from history mentioned on *The West Wing* include:

- Hubert Humphrey ("The Stackhouse Filibuster")
- Henry Clay ("The White House Pro-Am"
- William H. Seward ("Jefferson Lives")
- Aaron Burr ("Stirred")
- Alexander Hamilton ("The Leadership Breakfast")
- John C. Calhoun ("Han")
- Daniel Webster ("The Fall's Gonna Kill You")
- Henry Kissinger ("100,000 Airplanes")
- William Jennings Bryan ("The Black Vera Wang")
- George C. Marshall ("Somebody's Going to Emergency, Somebody's Going to Jail")
- Donald Rumsfeld ("The Short List")
- John Foster Dulles ("Pilot"

The Best of Will Bailey

"I like to think I have a certain flair."

~Will, "Inauguration, Pt. I" (S4/E14)

"Yeah. Can I tell you three things? You are more in need of a night in Atlantic City than any man I've ever met. Number two is, the last thing you need to worry about is no blood going there. You've got blood going there, about 13 ways. And some of it isn't good. Once again, I say, 'Atlantic City.' I'd say sit down at a table, go for dinner, see a show, take a walk on the boardwalk and smell the salt air... but if you're anything like me, nothing after 'sit down at a table' is going to happen."

~Will, to Toby, "Arctic Radar" (S4/E9)

"Millions of angry grandparents are going to march on Washington, burn us in effigy... thousands of grannies in walkers, tens of thousands of ancient veterans on oxygen, singing 'We Shall Overcome'!"

~Will, "Shutdown" (S5/E8)

"You know it occurs to me that if you ever used - and the fact that you haven't earns you major cliche avoidance points - the old, 'I could tell you but then I'd have to kill you' trope, that, given your background, you probably actually could... alarmingly alluring!"

~Will, "Running Mates" (S7/E10)

"I can't act! I'm a terrible actor!"

~Will, "Internal Displacement" (S7/E11)

Six Degrees of Abbey Bartlet

So Jed met Mrs. Landingham in prep school, where his dad was the headmaster and she was dad's secretary. That makes them the oldest connection in *The West Wing*, predating even his meeting Abbey at Notre Dame.

Jed then met Leo at some point in the next decade, but their friendship began in earnest around 20 years later. Leo was also good friends with Noah Lyman, father of Josh. So Leo knew Josh.

Somewhere in between, Abbey Bartlet babysat for a young Amy Gardner. Where she found time to do that, already having at least one daughter of her own and becoming a surgeon, is anybody's guess.

Josh pulled in Sam, and they clearly had been good friends for years – though Josh went to Harvard and Yale, while Sam went to Duke and Princeton. Maybe they met at Dungeons & Dragons camp.

Leo brought in Toby, and Toby had worked with CJ and convinced Leo she should come on board.

Charlie showed up to be a White House messenger (he had his own bike); and Donna just walked in off the street.

But here's where it gets squirrelly...

Abbey knew Amy from having babysat her; but she (Amy) was also "having quite a bit of sex with Chris", Josh's roommate at Yale. Put another way, Amy was babysat by the wife of the best-friend-to-be of the close friend of Josh's dad.[31]

Or, put yet another way, Amy was babysat by the wife of the best friend of the old friend of the father of the roommate of her future lover Chris.[32]

That's pushing plausibility *waaaayyy* too far, can't we agree?

But even if we grant this against-the-odds coincidence, we still have

---

[31] In Six Degrees of Separation terms, the connections above lead us not to Kevin Bacon, but full circle. Read on...

[32] Abbey -> Amy -> Josh -> Leo -> Jed -> (back to) Abbey,

or

Amy -> Abbey -> Jed -> Leo -> Josh -> (back to) Amy

some unanswered questions: how did Leo know Toby, so well that he wanted him on the campaign over and above Jed's homeboys and in spite of his love of bourbon?

And, if we're parsing coincidences – what are the odds that Leo's top-priority political operative's choice for press secretary had been doinked by the Senate boss of the son of Leo's old friend Noah?

Or, put another way, John Hoynes doinked the press-secretary-to-be selected by the political operative hired by the best friend of the husband of the woman who babysat the lover of the college roommate of Hoynes' staffer Josh.[33]

Let's get to the bottom of *that*...

~TWW~

Legitimate Dude Sightings

Like his peers Allison Janney, Richard Schiff and Brad Whitford, Dulé Hill went from *The West Wing* into a starring role on a new show. In his case, that show was *Psyche*, where he played Burton "Gus" Guster (he reprised the role in a TV movie). He was also in the cast of *The Wonder Years* (2021-23), and made guest appearances on *Suits*, *The Muppet Babies*, and a dozen other shows.

Josh Malina, that terrible actor, found a home as a series regular on *Scandal* as US Attorney David Rosen, and made recurring appearances on *The Big Bang Theory* as CalTech President Siebert. He also did guest spots on *House MD*, *Bones*, *Grey's Anatomy*, Dulé's *Psych*, Richard Schiff's *The Good Doctor*, *The Sarah Conner Chronicles*, *CSI: Crime Scene Investigation*, *iCarly*, *Stargate SG-1*, and others.

And, of course, he co-hosted *The West Wing Weekly* podcast for four years.

---

[33] Leo -> Toby -> CJ -> Hoynes -> Josh -> (back to) Leo,

or

Hoynes -> CJ -> Toby -> Leo -> Jed -> Abbey -> Amy -> Josh -> (back to) Hoynes

The Best of Season One

"We're running away from ourselves, and I know we can score points that way. I was the principal architect in that campaign strategy, right along with you, Josh. But we're here now. Tomorrow night, we do an immense thing. We have to say what we feel. That government, no matter what its failures are in the past, and in times to come, for that matter, the government can be a place where people come together and where no one gets left behind. *No one...* gets left behind! An instrument of good."

~Toby Ziegler, "He Shall, From Time to Time" (S1/E12)

"Twenties and Thirties, it was the role of government. Fifties and Sixties, it was civil rights. The next two decades, it's gonna be privacy. I'm talking about the Internet. I'm talking about cellphones. I'm talking about health records, and who's gay and who's not. And moreover, in a country born on a will to be free, what could be more fundamental than this?"

~Sam Seaborn, "The Short List" (S1/E6)

"Education is the silver bullet! Education is everything! We don't need little changes, we need gigantic, monumental changes! Schools should be palaces! The competition for the best teachers should be fierce! They should be making six-figure salaries! School should be incredibly expensive for government and absolutely free of charge to its citizens, just like national defense. That's my position. I just haven't figured out how to do it yet."

~Sam, "Six Meetings Before Lunch" (S1/E18)

"Don't go for the geniuses; they never want to sleep!"

~Abbey Bartlet, "He Shall, From Time to Time" (S1/E12)

"There is a connection between the progress of a society and progress in the Arts. The Age of Pericles was also the Age of Phidias. The Age of Lorenzo de Medici was also the Age of Leonardo Da Vinci. The Age of Elizabeth was the Age of Shakespeare."

~Toby, "Gone Quiet" (S3/E6)

"Andrew Jackson, in the main foyer of his White House had a big block of cheese. The block of cheese was huge – over two tons. And it was there for any and all who might be hungry. Jackson wanted the White House to belong to the people, so from time to time, he opened his doors to those who wished an audience."

~Leo McGarry, "The Crackpots and These Women" (S1/E5)

"You got a best friend? Is he smarter than you? Would you trust him with your life? That's your chief of staff..."

~Jed Bartlet, "He Shall, From Time to Time" (S1/E12)

"In a battle between a President's demons and his better angels, for the first time in a long while, I think we might just have ourselves a fair fight."

~Toby, "The Crackpots and These Women" (S1/E5)

"Just be wrong! Just stand there in your wrongness and be wrong, and get used to it!"

~"The White House Pro Am" (S1/E17)

"I drink from the keg of glory, Donna. Bring me the finest muffins and bagels in all the land!"

~"Post Hoc, Ergo Propter Hoc" (s1E2)

"In the meantime, a time when the public is rightly concerned about the impact of sex and violence on TV this administration is gonna protect the Muppets, we're gonna protect *Wall Street Week*, we're gonna protect *Live from Lincoln Center*, and by god, we are going to protect Julia Child!"

~"Take Out the Trash Day" (S1/E13)

"I miss my boys... Twins. Andrew and Simon. I tried not, you know, I dressed them differently, but they still did everything together. They went off to medical school together, and then they finished their second year at the same time, and of course their lottery number came up at the same time... they wanted to go where people needed doctors. Their father and I begged them, but you can't tell kids anything. So they joined up as medics and four months later they were pinned down during a fight in DaNang and were killed by enemy fire. That was Christmas Eve 1970. You know, they were so young, Charlie, they were your age. It's hard when that happens so far away, you know because, with the noises and the shooting, they had to be so scared. It's hard not to think that right then they needed their mother... Anyway, I miss my boys."

~Mrs. Landingham, "In Excelsis Deo" (S1/E10)

"Decisions are made by those who show up!"

~Jed Bartlet, "What Kind of Day Has It Been?" (S1/E22)

~TWW~

Real-world political activists mentioned on *The West Wing*:

- Martin Luther King, Jr. ("College Kids")
- Gloria Steinem ("17 People")
- Naomi Wolf ("17 People")
- Phyllis Schlafley ("17 People", "20 Hours in America")

The Best of Season Two

"Today, for the first time in history, one in five Americans living in poverty are children. One in five children live in the most abject, dangerous, hopeless, backbreaking, gut-wrenching, poverty, one in five, and they're children. If fidelity to freedom and democracy is the code of our civic religion, then surely, the code of our humanity is faithful service to that unwritten commandment that says, 'We shall give our children better than we ourselves had.' I voted against the bill 'cause I didn't want it to be hard for people to buy milk. I stopped some money from flowing into your pocket. If that angers you, if you resent me, I completely respect that, but if you expect anything different from the President of the United States, I suggest you vote for somebody else."

~Jed Bartlet, "In the Shadow of Two Gunmen" (S2/E1)

"Because I'm tired of it, year after year after year after year! Having to choose between the lesser of who cares? Of trying to get myself excited about a candidate who can speak in complete sentences! Of setting the bar so low, I can hardly look at it. They say a good man can't get elected President. I don't believe that, do you?

~"In the Shadow of Two Gunmen, Pt. I" (S2/E1)

"Tonight, what began on the commons in Concord, Massachusetts, as an alliance of farmers and workers, of cobbles man and tinsmiths, of statesmen and students, of mothers and wives, of men and boys, lives two centuries later as America! My name is Josiah Bartlet, and I accept your nomination for the Presidency of the United States!"

~Jed Bartlet, "In the Shadow of Two Gunmen, Pt. II" (S2/E2)

"The President likes smart people who disagree with him... the

President's asking you to serve – and everything else is crap!"
~Leo, "In This White House" (S2/E4)

"Say they're smug and superior, say their approach to public policy makes you want to tear your hair out. Say they like high taxes and spending your money. Say they want to take your guns and open your borders - but don't call them worthless. At least, don't do it in front of me.
"The people that I have met have been extraordinarily qualified! Their intent is good, their commitment is true. They are righteous, and they are patriots. And I'm their lawyer."
~Ainsley, "In This White House" (S2/E4)

"Nobody expects, nobody expects! Toby, it seems to me that more and more we've come to expect less and less from each other. And I think that should change."
~Sen. Tony Marino, "The Lame Duck Congress" (S2E6)

"[We really need to go to Mars] 'cause it's next! 'Cause we came out of the cave, and we looked over the hill, and we saw fire! And we crossed the ocean, and we pioneered the West, and we took to the sky! The history of man is hung on the timeline of exploration, and this is what's next!"
~Sam, "Galileo" (S2/E9)

"[The painting] was on loan from the Musee d'Orsay to the National Gallery. The President, on a visit to the gallery, and possessing even less taste in fine art than you have in accessories, announced that he liked the painting. The French government offered it as a gift to the White House, I suppose in retribution for EuroDisney. So here it hangs, like a gym sock on a shower rod."
~Bernard Thatch, "Noël" (S2/E10)

"This guy's walking down a street, when he falls in a hole. The walls are so steep, he can't get out. A doctor passes by, and the guy shouts up, 'Hey you! Can you help me out?' The doctor writes him a prescription, throws it down the hole and moves on. Then a priest comes along, and the guy shouts up 'Father, I'm down in this hole, can you help me out?' The priest writes out a prayer, throws it down in the hole and moves on. Then a friend walks by. 'Hey Joe, it's me, can you help me out?' And the friend jumps in the hole! Our guy says 'Are you stupid? Now we're both down here!' and the friend says, 'Yeah, but I've been down here before, and I know the way out.'"

~"Noël" (S2/E10)

"You're a son of a bitch, you know that? She bought her first new car and you hit her with a drunk driver. What, was that supposed to be funny? 'You can't conceive, nor can I, the appalling strangeness of the mercy of God,' says Graham Greene. I don't know whose ass he was kissing there, 'cause I think you're just vindictive. What was Josh Lyman? A warning shot? That was my son. What did I ever do to yours except praise his glory and praise his name? There's a tropical storm that's gaining speed and power. They say we haven't had a storm this bad since you took out the tender ship of mine last year in the North Atlantic last year... 68 crew! Do you know what a tender ship does? Fixes the other ships! Doesn't even carry guns! Floats around and fixes the other ships and delivers the mail. That's all it can do. *Gratias tibi ago, domine.* Yes, I lied! It was a sin! I've committed many sins! Have I displeased you, you feckless thug? Three-point-eight million new jobs, that wasn't good? Bailed out Mexico, increased foreign trade, 30 million new acres for conservation, put Mendoza on the bench, we're not fighting a war, I've raised three children... That's not enough to buy me out of the doghouse? *Haec credam a deo pio? A deo iusto? A deo scito? Cruciatus in crucem! Tuus in terra servus, nuntius fui; officium perfeci Cruciatus in crucem. Eas in crucem!*

"You get Hoynes!"

~Jed Bartlet, "Two Cathedrals" (S2/E22)

~TWW~

There is in fact no traffic light at the intersection of 18th and Potomac in Washington, DC.

~TWW~

In "Celestial Navigation", Josh has a coffee mug with the logo of Wesleyan University on it. In "Manchester, Pt. II", Josh wears a Wesleyan University t-shirt. But Josh didn't go to Wesleyan; he went to Harvard and Yale.
Brad Whitford went to Wesleyan.

~TWW~

Places that exist in WestWingWorld but not in the real world:

- San Andrea, CA ("Duck and Cover")
- Kennison State University ("20 Hours in America", "College Kids")
- Hartsfield's Landing ("Hartsfield's Landing")
- The Equatorial Republic of Kundu ("In This White House", etc.)
- Qumar ("The Women of Qumar", etc.)

~TWW~

Tom Merrill, mentioned by Toby but unseen in "Institutional Memory", is a real person - a legal scholar, a professor at Columbia Law School. Toby tells CJ that he called Merrill to inquire about whether or not the smudge of law he found in the original Constitution changes the meaning of the takings clause.

Bartlet Baby Math

If the timetable of Matt Santos's public service is not altogether credible, the reproductive history of Jed and Abbey Bartlet is even more challenged.

The Bartlets, of course, have three daughters – Liz, Ellie, and Zoey. And we are given useful biographical facts right up front, in the pilot episode, when Jed Bartlet informs some visiting Christians that Liz's precocious daughter Annie is all of 12 – which puts Liz's age somewhere in the early 30s.

Except...

Jed tells Charlie, not long after that (in "Five Votes Down"), that he and Abbey have been married for 32 years – meaning Annie was born around their 20th anniversary.

Which means one of two things: 1) either Liz was born before her parents were married, or 2) Liz and her pinhead husband Doug got busy and produced Annie while they were still teenagers.

We know that the senior Bartlets have a combined age of 111 in the sixth year of the Bartlet presidency ("Slow News Day") and are close to the same age, based on attending adjacent colleges at the same time. This puts them in both in the 55-57 age range[34] when "Slow News Day" occurs – and knocking six years off those ages, they were in their late 40s when Jed assumed office.

Take 32 years off that, and we have them conceiving Liz while still teenagers.

That seems pretty scandalous for two Catholic students in Catholic college in 1967, but the math doesn't leave us anywhere else to go! So we must move on and accept that Jed figured out a way to get his tight-ass father to sign off on such an early marriage.

Liz and Doug are, of course, in exactly the same boat: assuming she was born in wedlock, she must have been 20, at the very most, when Annie was born – and now we have to wonder how she got *her* tight-ass father to sign off on such an early marriage!

---

[34] ...with an age split of 55-56, 54-57, or 53-58 at most – with Abbey's pregnancy getting all the more scandalous, regardless of which is older, the farther apart they are.

Then again, we know that the Bartlet women tend to be a little randy – Abbey says it outright in "And It's Surely to Their Credit"! – and there's that awkward question... why, again, do Ellie and Vic have to get married right away?

~TWW~

We all remember that shocking moment when Charlie answers the phone, looks stricken by what he hears, then slowly hangs up and reports to Leo, who's standing there at his desk, that Mrs. Landingham has been in a car accident.

"Charlie, is she all right?" Leo asks, alarmed.

"No," Charlie replies, "She's dead."[35]

Melissa Fitzgerald and Mary McCormack reveal in *What's Next* that the table read for this episode was a shock. Why? Because the cast had their scripts for the episode and it had been discussed – but someone was still out of the loop.

"Everyone prior to the table read had been told Mrs. Landingham was going to die... except Dulé," Aaron Sorkin is quoted. So the cast is reading the script aloud, and they all arrive at that fateful phone call – and it so happens that Charlie's reply to Leo is at the top of the next page. He turns the page and sees the words, "She's dead." And he didn't know it was coming.

"The poor kid," Sorkin said. "Honestly, we weren't pranking him. It was just one of those 'I thought you told him-' 'I thought *you* told him kinds of things."

Fitzgerald and McCormack bring the point home: "Yes," they wrote, "thanks to that miscommunication between Aaron and Tommy, Dulé was left to live through Delores Landingham's death right there in front of the whole gang – including Kathryn herself."

---

[35] In "18th and Potomac", S2/E21.

The Best of Season Three

"Leo, we need to be investigated by someone who wants to kill us just to watch us die! We need someone perceived by the American people to be irresponsible, untrustworthy, partisan, ambitious and thirsty for the limelight. Am I crazy or is this not a job for the US House of Representatives?"

~CJ, "Ways and Means" (S3/E3)

"There's an old saying: 'Those who speak, don't know; and those who know, don't speak.' I don't know if that's true or not, but I know that by and large, the press doesn't care who really knows what as long as they've got a quote.

"Last Friday, we had our Week Ahead meeting in the Roosevelt Room. Some of you were there, most of you weren't, but I'm talking to all of you now. Bruno Gianelli and I were leading a discussion about whether or not the President should stop in Kansas on his way back from the West Coast, and I remarked that the Vice President is polling better than the President right now in the Plains states - and that if the President is re-elected, it's gonna be on the Vice President's coattails. That remark made its way to a White House reporter.

"We're a group. We're a team. From the President and Leo on through, we're a team. We win together, we lose together, we celebrate and we mourn together. And defeats are softened and victories sweetened because we did them together. And if you don't like this team - then, there's the door. It's great to be in the know. It's great to have the scoop, to have the skinny, to be able to go to a reporter and say, 'I know something you don't know.' And so the press becomes your constituents and you sell out the team.

"...I'm not gonna have a witch hunt. I'm not gonna huff and puff. I'm not gonna take anyone's head off. I'm simply gonna say this: you're my guys. And I'm yours. And there's nothing I wouldn't do for you."

~Toby, "War Crimes" (S3/E5)

"There is a connection between progress of a society and progress in the Arts. The Age of Pericles was also the Age of Phidias. The Age of Lorenzo de Medici was also the Age of Leonardo Da Vinci. The Age of Elizabeth was the Age of Shakespeare."

~"Gone Quiet" (S3/E6)

"I am tired of working for candidates who make me think I should be embarrassed to believe what I believe, Sam! I'm tired of getting them elected! We all need some therapy, because somebody came along and said 'liberal' means 'soft on crime, soft on drugs, soft on communism, soft on defense, and we're gonna tax you back to the Stone Age, because people shouldn't have to go to work if they don't want to!' And instead of saying, 'Well, excuse me, you right-wing, reactionary, xenophobic, homophobic, anti-education, anti-choice, pro-gun, Leave-It-to-Beaver trip back to the Fifties!' - we cowered in the corner and said, 'Please, don't hurt me!' No more! I really don't care who's right, who's wrong. We're both right! We're both wrong! Let's have two parties, huh? What do you say?"

~Bruno Gianelli, "Gone Quiet" (S3/E6)

"Nature is to be protected from. Nature, much like a woman, will seduce you with its sights, its scents and its touch. And then it breaks your ankle. Also like a woman."

~Oliver Babish, "Gone Quiet" (S3/E6)

"I was wrong! I was. I was just... I was wrong! Come on, you know that! Lots of times we don't know what right or wrong is, but lots of times we do and come on, this is one! I may not have had sinister intent at the outset, but there were plenty of opportunities for me to make it right. No one in government takes responsibility for anything anymore. We foster, we obfuscate, we rationalize. 'Everybody does it.' That's what we say. so we come to occupy a moral safe house where everyone's to blame so no one's guilty. I'm to blame. I was wrong!"

~Jed Bartlet, "H. Con - 172" (S3/E10)

"Outraged? I'm barely surprised. This is a country where women aren't allowed to drive a car. They're not allowed to be in the company of any man other than a close relative; they're required to adhere to a dress code that would make the Maryknoll Nun look like Malibu Barbie. They beheaded 121 people last year for robbery, rape, and drug trafficking, they've no free press, no elected government, no political parties, and the royal family allows the religious police to travel in groups of six, carrying nightsticks and they freely and publicly beat women. But 'Brutus is an honorable man.'

"Seventeen schoolgirls were forced to burn alive because they weren't wearing the proper clothing. Am I outraged? No, Steve. No Chris. No, Mark. That is Saudi Arabia, our partners in peace. Bonnie, then Scott."

~CJ, "Enemies Foreign and Domestic" (S3/E18)

"Can you tell when it's peacetime and wartime anymore? I don't know who the world's leading expert on welfare is, but any list of the top has got to include me, and I can't tell when it's peacetime and wartime anymore!

"We measure the success of a mission by two things: was it successful and how few civilians did we hurt. They measure success by how many! Pregnant women are delivering bombs! You're talking to me about international laws? The laws of *nature* don't even apply here! I've been a soldier for 38 years! And I found an enemy I can kill. He can't cancel Shareef's trip, Leo! You've got to tell him he can't cancel it!"

~Admiral Percy Fitzwallace, "We Killed Yamamoto" (S3/E20)

~TWW~

Prof. Lawrence Lessig, played by Christopher Lloyd in "The Wake Up Call", is a real person; he is a legal scholar and political activist at Harvard University. He was briefly a candidate for the Democratic presidential nomination in 2016.

Who said that? (Round 2)

1.   "'Mothers are standing in front of tanks.' And we're going to go get their backs."

____

2.   "All through history, no one's wanted either of them."

____

3.   "With the clothes on their backs, they came through a storm."

____

4.   "It's the only country left in the world where it's impossible to access the Internet."

____

5.   "International law has no prohibition against any government, superpower or otherwise, targeting terrorist command and control centers. And Abdul Shareef was a walking command and control center."

____

6.   "Doesn't this mean we join the league of ordinary nations?"

____

7.   "That is Saudi Arabia – our partners in peace."

____

8.   "You really want to reach in and kill them where they live?
Keep accepting more than one idea. Makes 'em absolutely crazy!"

____

9.   "Look at the whole board..."

____

10.   "Mexico's on fire. Why help them? Because we can."

____

Who Said That? (Round 2) Answers

1. President Bartlet
2. Kate Harper
3. President Bartlet
4. CJ
5. Acting President Glen Allen Walken
6. President Bartlet
7. CJ
8. Josh
9. President Bartlet
10. Josh

~TWW~

Legitimate Dude Sightings

Janel Moloney followed up *The West Wing* with many guest spots on television, on *House, 30 Rock, Law & Order: Criminal Intent, The Good Wife, Law & Order: Special Victims Unit, Bull, Law & Order: Organized Crime*, among others.

She's also made a few film appearances, most notably in *The Leisure Seeker* (2017), with Donald Sutherland and Helen Mirren.

Mary McCormack showed up playing an FBI agent on Aaron Sorkin's *The Newsroom*, but showed up plenty of other places as well; on the big screen, she was in *K-PAX*, the Stephen King horror film *1408*, the Christopher Guest mockumentary *For Your Consideration*, and about a dozen others.

On TV, she appeared on *Law & Order: Criminal Intent, Scandal*, the revived *Will & Grace*, and many others.

The Best of Season Four

"More than any time in recent history, America's destiny is not of our own choosing. We did not seek, nor did we provoke an assault on our freedom and our way of life. We did not expect, nor did we invite a confrontation with evil. Yet the true measure of a people's strength is how they rise to master that moment when it does arrive. 44 people were killed a couple of hours ago at Kennison State University. Three swimmers from the men's team were killed and two others are in critical condition. When, after having heard the explosion from their practice facility, they ran into the fire to help get people out. Ran *into* the fire.

"The streets of heaven are too crowded with angels tonight. They're our students and our teachers and our parents and our friends. The streets of heaven are too crowded with angels, but every time we think we have measured our capacity to meet a challenge, we look up and we're reminded that that capacity may well be limitless. This is a time for American heroes! We will do what is hard; we will achieve what is great. This is a time for American heroes, and we reach for the stars! God bless their memory, God bless you, and God bless the United State of America! Thank you."

~Jed Bartlet, "20 Hours in America" (S4/E1)

"This is Ms. Cregg. She's the White House Press Secretary and senior counsel to the President. And if she wasn't, she would still be Ms. Cregg! I don't mind you not respecting people. I mind you doing it out loud. I mind you doing it in this building. You wanna be a punk, fine, but I don't think you've got the size for it. You wanna go to juvie, get out, deal, and kill cops? Okay, but every time you do a crime, you get caught, so I think you're gonna have to do something else. 9:00 on Saturday mornings, I eat breakfast at Cosmo's on Delaware. I come here for an hour and do office work, and then I go to St. Jude's for an hour to play basketball. You can go to juvie, or you can be at Cosmo's

9:00 on Saturday morning. It's entirely up to you."
~Charlie, "20 Hours in America" (S4/E1)

"I am not kidding. I have such an impulse to knock your heads together! I can't remember the last time I heard you two talk about anything other than how a campaign was playing in Washington. Cathy needed to take a second job so her dad could be covered by her insurance. She tried to tell you how bad things were for family farmers. You told her we already lost Indiana. You made fun of the fair, but you didn't see they have livestock exhibitions and give prizes for the biggest tomato and the best heirloom apple. They're proud of what they grow. Eight modes of transportation, the kindness of six strangers, random conversations with 12 more, and nobody brought up Bartlet versus Ritchie but you. I'm writing letters on your behalf to the parents of the kids who were killed today. Can I have the table, please?
~Donna, to Josh and Toby, "20 Hours in America" (S4/E1)

"'Joy cometh in the morning,' scripture tells us. I hope so. I don't know if life would be worth living if it didn't. And I don't yet know who set off the bomb at Kennison State. I don't know if it's one person or 10, and I don't know what they want. All I know for sure, all I know for certain, is that they weren't born wanting to do this. There's evil in the world. There'll always be, and we can't do anything about that. But there's violence in our schools, too much mayhem in our culture, and we *can* do something about that! There's not enough character, discipline, and depth in our classrooms. There aren't enough teachers in our classrooms. There isn't nearly enough, not nearly enough, not *nearly* enough money in our classrooms, and we can do something about that! We're not doing nearly enough, not nearly enough to teach our children well! And we can do better, and we must do better, and we *will* do better! And we will start this moment today! They weren't born wanting to do this!"
~Jed Bartlet, "College Kids" (S4/E2)

"'I believe in hope, not fear!' 'I'm a leader, not a politician!' 'It's time for an American leader!' 'America's earned a change!' 'I before E except

after C!' It's the fortune cookie candidacy! [Kant and Plato] are important thinkers, and understanding them can be very useful and it's not ever going to happen at a four-hour seminar. When the President's got an embassy surrounded in Haiti, or a keyhole photograph of a heavy water reactor, or any of the 50 life-and-death matters that walk across his desk every day, I don't know if he's thinking about Immanuel Kant or not. I doubt it, but if he does, I am comforted at least in my certainty that he is doing his best to reach for *all* of it, and not just the McNuggets! Is it possible we would be willing to require any less of the person sitting in that chair? The low road? I don't think it is!"

~Josh, "The Red Mass" (S4/E3)

"'Free trade is essential for human rights...' The end of that sentence is, '...we hope, because nothing else has worked.' The President knows Chinese political prisoners are going to be sewing soccer balls with their teeth whether we sell them cheeseburgers or not, so let's sell them cheeseburgers."

~Asst. Secretary of State Albie Duncan, "Game On" (S4/E5)

"You know, you get a pretty good aerobic workout talking to

someone in this building."
~Will, "Guns Not Butter" (S4/E11)

"Why is a Kundunese life worth less to me than an American life?"
~Jed Bartlet, "Inauguration, Pt. I" (S4/E13)

"'Fear of cancer from asbestos,
Fuzzy science manifestos'

'Guilty
or not guilty,
past convictions frustrate
the judge who wonders should your fate
abate.'"
~Leo, "Inauguration, Pt. I" (S4/E13)

"'I say this denial
Is not fit for trial!'"
~Leo, "Inauguration: Over There" (S4/E14)

"Well, the problem is, and you weren't to be told beforehand, but Mrs. Bartlet, during the presentation of honors this evening, was to personally present you with an award... It's for your many years of service. It's a key. The Francis Scott Key. It's the Francis Scott Key Key."
~Amy Gardner, "Privateers" (S4/E17)

"You know, a friend of mine's a comedian, and he was doing a standup here in town. A bunch of people from the German consulate came down to see him, and they came backstage afterwards, and they said to him, 'How come we don't have anyone as funny as you back

home?' And my friend said, 'Because you killed them all.'"
~Congressman Tom Landis, "Angle Maintenance" (S4/E18)

"Yes, Joe. The girls in the Political Affairs Office saw you before and asked me to tell you that they wouldn't have covered your parking spot with mayonnaise if they'd known you were a biscuit."
~Margaret, to Joe Quincy, "Life on Mars" (S4/E20)

"I didn't realize babies come with hats. You guys crack me up! You don't have jobs. You can't walk or speak the language. You don't have a dollar in your pockets, but you got yourselves a hat. So, everything's fine. I don't wanna alarm you or anything, but I'm Dad. And for you, son, for you, this'll be the last time I pass the buck, but I think it should be clear from the get-go that it was Mom who named you Huckleberry. I guess she was feeling like life doesn't present enough challenges to overcome on its own. And, honey, you've got a name now too. Your mom and I named you after an incredibly brave woman, really not all that much older than you. Your name is Molly. Huck and Molly.
"So, what do I do? Well, you're gonna need food and clothes and doctors and dentists, and there's that. And should you have any questions along the way, I'm gonna be doin' stuff like this... Huck, because you're leaking a little bit out of your mouth there. You're holding my finger, son? Hey, Molly. Your brother's holding my hand. Do you wanna hold my hand? This isn't gonna mean anything to you, but Leo was right. Leo was right."
~"Twenty-Five" (S4/E22)

~TWW~

Josh cites "Mohammed al-Mohammed al-Mohammed bin Basir" as a stereotypical name for a terrorist in "20 Hours in America". In the later Sorkinverse series The *Newsroom*, the name is used again, prompting Jeff Daniels' Roy McAvoy character to ask, "Fox hired someone with three Mohammeds in their name?"

~TWW~

Legitimate Dude Sightings

Kristin Chenowith is notable as an accomplished singer, and after her *West Wing* stint, she had the opportunity to make the most of it on television in *Glee!*, where she had a recurring role, as well as *Pushing Daisies*, where she pulled in two Emmy nominations as Olive Snook.

She also had a recurring role on *The Good Wife* as political reporter Peggy Byrne, and popped up on the big screen as Fifi, Snoopy's love interest in *The Peanuts Movie*, and in *The Boy Next Door, National Champions*, and others.

From West Wing to *West Wing*

Above, we noted with interest that Aaron Sorkin's *The American President*, the prototype for *The West Wing*, passed five of its actors on to the series: Martin Sheen, Anna Deavere Smith, Josh Malina, Nina Siemaszko, Ralph Meyering, Jr., Ron Canada, and Thom Barry.

That's a pretty impressive tally – but it's nothing compared to another White House-based movie that was released just after *The West Wing itself*. It had even more *West Wing* actors than *The American President*.

Thirteen Days, directed by Roger Donaldson and starring Kevin Costner and Bruce Greenwood, was a dramatization of the Cuban Missile Crisis of 1962 based on Robert Kennedy's book. The two-week tussle between the US and the Soviet Union in October 1962 is seen through the eyes of Kennedy Special Assistant Kenny O'Donnell (Costner), who helps JFK (Greenwood) work through the events that took the world to the brink of nuclear horror.

There's a *West Wing* alum at the top of the cast – Steven Culp, who plays Bobby Kennedy, and went on to play Speaker of the House Jeff Haffley on *TWW* in the post-Sorkin years.[36]

And a number of others:

- Dylan Baker, who plays Secretary of Defense Robert McNamara, was Attorney General Alan Fisk in "Abu el Banat";
- Peter White – CIA Director John McCone in *Thirteen Days* – was Sam Seaborn's boss, the Gage in Gage-Whitney, in "In the Shadow of Two Gunmen";
- The famous character actor Elya Baskin, familiar as a Russian on both film and television, played Soviet Ambassador Anatoly Dobrynin, going on to play Mr. Zubatov, one of the representatives from Belarus who takes over the Roosevelt Room to write a constitution

---

[36] Martin Sheen also played Bobby Kennedy, in the TV movie *The Missiles of October* (1974).

with the help of Christopher Lloyd in "The Wake Up Call";
- Dakin Matthews, Arthur Lundahl in *Thirteen Days*, played Leo's old friend Simon Blye, out to sink him with an op-ed in "Take Out the Trash Day";
- John Aylward, portraying *New York Times* publisher Orvil Dryfoos, was also DNC operative Barry Goodwin in TWW's 6th and 7th seasons;
- Michael Gaston, playing the captain of the *USS Pierce* on the Cuban blockade line in *Thirteen Days*, was Josh Lyman's frustrated classmate Eric Hayden, holding out for a federal bench posting in "Eppur Si Muove";
- And finally, there's Tom Everett in the role of FBI Agent Walter Sheridan in *Thirteen Days* – back to irritate Kate Harper as Charles Frost in "Message of the Week", "Mr. Frost", and "Here Today".

~TWW~

Legitimate Dude Sightings

Before his 2005 death in *The West Wing*'s sixth season, John Spencer was well known as Tommy Mullaney on *LA Law*. But he also popped up in a great many other places:

- He debuted as a teenager on *The Patty Duke Show*;
- He appeared in the movie *War Games* (1983) as an Air Force captain;
- He did some soap opera, appearing on *Ryan's Hope, Another World* and *As the World Turns*;
- He co-starred in the Harrison Ford legal thriller *Presumed Innocent* (1990) alongside a young Brad Whitford;
- He played FBI Director James Womack alongside Sean Connery in *The Rock* (1996);
- He made guest appearances on *Miami Vice, Spenser: For Hire, Touched by an Angel, Lois & Clark: The New Adventures of Superman* and others.

The Best of Season Five

"You know I'm not the enemy. The things that unite us are far greater than things that divide us. We both believe in democracy, preservation of American values, protection of our citizens in a sometimes-hostile world."

~Glen Allen Walken, to CJ,
"7A WF 83429" (S5/E1)

"'The Lord giveth and the Lord taketh away.' -Words I did not fully understand until our daughter was taken from us three days ago. But now we can rejoice and be glad, for that which was lost has been found. That my child is back in her mother's arms is serendipity and grace; a second chance that will not slip through our hands again. I wish I could tell you there's some new policy, some new weapons system - a silver bullet, perhaps - that could meet this moment; that could keep us safe from the terror that's now among us. But if I were to say that, I'd be lying. All I can promise is that I will fight with every fiber of my being, every weapon in our arsenal, and with every ounce of God's grace..."

~Jed Bartlet, "The Dogs of War" (S5/E2)

"Here's another good one: 'Dear Zoey, I hope they don't kill you. But if they do, that it'll be quick.'"

~Zoey, "Jefferson Lives" (S5/E3)

"Two hundred twenty-seven years ago, a bunch of guys got together on the 4th of July and decided, because they didn't have any cherry

bombs, they would declare some self-evident truths."
~Jed Bartlet, "Jefferson Lives" (S5/E3)

"Mrs. Bartlet, I can't tell you how hard I prayed for you... I'm not very religious, so there's the risk that my praying could be taken as insincere or even an affront, which, if it's a vengeful God, could have made matters worse."
~Debbie Fiderer, "Jefferson Lives" (S5/E3)

"What a waste, since the moon. My generation never got the future it was promised. 35 years later, cars, air travel's the same. We don't even have the Concorde anymore. Technology stopped. [The personal computer:} A more efficient delivery system for gossip and pornography. Where's my jet pack, my colonies on the Moon? Just a waste!"
~"The Warfare of Genghis Khan" (s5/E13)

"Voyager, in case it's ever encountered by extraterrestrials, is carrying photos of life on Earth, greetings in 55 languages, and a collection of music from Gregorian chants to Chuck Berry - including 'Dark Was The Night, Cold Was The Ground' by '20s bluesman Blind Willie Johnson, whose stepmother blinded him when he was seven by throwing lye in is his eyes after his father had beaten her for being with another man. He died, penniless, of pneumonia after sleeping bundled in wet newspapers in the ruins of his house that burned down.
"But his music just left the solar system."
~Josh, "The Warfare of Genghis Khan" (S5/E13)

"No, the President has no intention of starting a worldwide bra war. I really don't think the President would ever start a war that the French might actually win."

~"Full Disclosure" (S5/E15)

"While money spent studying the brains of PCP users might seem to be taxpayer waste, this research led directly to the discovery of the NMDA receptor. Science cannot exist in a vacuum. By nature, it's an open enterprise, strengthened by public scrutiny.

"Openness is the basis of a free society. But when science is attacked on ideological grounds, its integrity and usefulness are threatened. Independent peer-reviewed research is the cornerstone of science in America. It shouldn't be about the left or the right, but what works to keep people safe and healthy. I believe all Americans and all people everywhere, no matter who they are or how they live, deserve research to improve their lives. Thomas Jefferson said, 'We must not be afraid to follow the truth wherever it may lead.' Scientific truth ennobles us. It tells us who we are, where we've been, and where we're going. I believe the truth will only be found when all scientists are free to pursue it. Thank you."

~Ellie, "Eppur Si Muove" (S5/E16)

"Go ahead, see who they pick of their favorite sons! See what segregationists, anti-miscegenationist, Isaiah-quoting, gay-bashing bastard they come up with! Jed Bartlet - from New Hampshire! - had an idea!"

~Chief Justice Roy Ashland, "The Supremes" (S5/17)

"Do you know what this lifestyle does to the body? The minute your system senses stress, it releases a hormone that constricts the blood vessels, contracts the heart muscles, stimulates the adrenal gland! You stay in this state for not a hundredth of the time that you and I have existed like this, and the vessels begin to shred; the heart permanently constricts; the intestines, the immune system shut down. Relieving those conditions is the one responsible course of action I can take! I am sorry it is not a course of action that's available to you, but if you think you're going to talk me out of it with some Valley of the Dolls cautionary tale, you have picked the wrong girl!"

~Abbey, to Leo, "No Exit" (S5/20)

"In 75 years, we'll know whether we're right or wrong, but no one standing here today can tell me that with any certainty. I'm the one in the office. I'll be the one who's judged."

~Jed Bartlet, "Memorial Day" (S5/22)

The Nixon Nexus

A great many real-world presidents are mentioned in *The West Wing*, and they're listed above. And the fictional Jed Bartlet also has a few fictional predecessors in WestWingWorld (Presidents Lassiter and Newman).

Where does the real universe branch off into the Sorkinverse?

The relatively recent presidencies that are part of WestWingWorld include John F. Kennedy – hard to leave him out, not just because he's so quotable, but because his name is attached to the Kennedy Center, Kennedy International Airport, the Kennedy School of Government, and so on. And we have an indirect reference to Lyndon Johnson – the Johnson Space Center, which is named for him, is mentioned in "Galileo".

Mandy mentions Richard Nixon by name in "Six Meetings Before Lunch", and Toby makes a more backward-reaching reference to him with the phrase "Eisenhower-Nixon" – a reference to a Fifties question about vice presidents being dropped from the ticket – to Leo in "17 People". Oliver Babish invokes Nixon indirectly in perhaps the most poignant way when a tape recording device in his office is stuck in Record, commenting, "...there's never been a problem with *that* before."[37]

The divergence of the *West Wing* timeline from the real world appears to occur at that point – after the Nixon presidency, which would be followed in WestWingWorld by President Bartlet's fictional predecessors, and a few more we never heard about.

Except...

Even though he's never mentioned, Ronald Reagan made it into WestWingWorld. When Toby approached Agent Ron Butterfield to try to take responsibility for the President's open-air policy at public appearances, they are standing in front of the Ronald Reagan Institute of Emergency Medicine ("In the Shadow of Two Gunmen, Pt. II"). By extension, Gerald Ford and Jimmy Carter are necessarily now part of WestWingWorld.

---

[37] In "Bad Moon Rising".

This puts us in a timeline crunch. If the timelines diverge after Reagan, that leaves a single decade before the Bartlet Administration began (and remember that presidential terms shifted two years in WestWingWorld, with Bartlet being elected in 1998 and 2002 – why, we never learned). That leaves time for two single-term presidencies and a couple of extra years accounting for the shift in terms.

Well, we know that President D. Wire Newman, a Democrat who preceded President Bartlet in WestWingWorld, was a one-term president, because he told us so ("The Stormy Present"). He would necessarily have immediately followed Ronald Reagan, as the presidency preceding Bartlet's was a Republican one (both Leo and Republican VP nominee Ray Sullivan refer to the Democrats having been in control of the White House for as long as President Bartlet has occupied it; Donna meets her predecessor, who is a Republican).

And this means that Leo was Secretary of Labor under Republican President Owen Lassiter (whose death is noted in "The Stormy Present"), as he was in the Cabinet from roughly 1993 to roughly 1997, when he would have necessarily left it to organize the first Bartlet campaign.

Leo was respected on both sides of the aisle, so that doesn't seem too far from the realm of the possible.

To summarize, Nixon's is the last real-world president's name actually spoken on *The West Wing* – but our eyes tell us the split comes 15 years later.

~TWW~

Foo Fighters appear and perform in "Election Day". They are also the band playing in the Georgetown bar where Josh and Sam take Charlie (and Zoey and CJ tag along) in "Mr. Willis of Ohio". The song is "Learn to Fly".

The Best of Season Six

"I was born in the city of Safra. Do you know Safra? It's in the mountains of Habrigaly. I was eight years old when the leaders left. There were 52 Arabs in Safra, but only a thousand, three hundred Jews. Within a month, the Haganah had taken over the city. My eldest sister, Amira, was killed. The body of my brother, Aziz, was found hanging from a burned Cyprus tree. We fled to Syria; lived in tents, ate the United Nations handouts and surplus American cheese. I still remember the view of the valley from the roof of our house; the smell of the pomegranates; the sound of children playing in our orchard. The home of my father, of my aunts and uncles, they are now art galleries and bed-and-breakfasts. Will I get to go home, Ms. Harper?"

~Palestinian Chairman Nizar Farad, "The Birnam Wood" (S6/2)

"I spent the last 14 hours being snickered at by United States senators, being ostracized on the World Wide Web, having my own colleagues question my ability to do my job, and I let it get to me. So I don't think it really matters whether I'm gay or straight, or just the best damn women's basketball player in Ohio Valley history. No one should be treated this way."

~CJ, "Faith Based Initiative" (S6/E10)

"I wanted to start this journey in the place where it all started for me. Soon, we will be inundated by the polls and the punditry and the prognostications - all the nonsense that goes with our national political campaigns. Well, none of that matters; *this* is the place that matters! Because every day, children walk into this schoolhouse to glimpse their futures, to ask for hope. They may not know they need it yet, but they do. And I'm here to tell you that hope is real. In a life of trials, in a world of challenges - hope is real. In a country where families go without health care, where some go without food, some don't even have a home to speak of - hope is real. In a time of global chaos and instability, where our faiths collide as often as our weapons – hope is real.

"Hope is what gives us the courage to take on our greatest challenges, to move forward together. We live in cynical times, I know that. But hope is not up for debate. There is such a thing as false science, there's such a thing as false promises. I am sure that I'll have my share of false starts in this campaign. But there is no such thing as false hope. There is only hope. And with your help and your hard work and the hopes of good people all across this land, I hereby announce my candidacy for President of these United States."

~Matt Santos, "Faith Based Initiative" (S6/E10)

"We rubes can throw down!"

~Annabeth, "365 Days" (S6/E12)

"My niece loves the M&M's with the Seal of the President. She takes them to school, gets a lot of attention. Got any of those around?"

~Cliff Calley, "Drought Conditions" (S6/E16)

"You know, when I got out of the Marines, I hadn't been around my old neighborhood in Houston in a few years. I had just gotten this job offer from the Pentagon, and it required a full FBI background check. After a few weeks, the investigators - they came up to me, and they said, 'We can't give you the job. We've interviewed all your old friends and neighbors. They can't confirm anything, not even your name.' So I hop a plane, go back to the old block. I see my neighbor's 11- and 13-year-old kids. They're sitting on the stoop, same as always, and they see me coming. They start running toward me, and they're shouting, 'Tío Matt, Tío Matt!' - Uncle Matt – 'Tío Matt, "the Feds- they were here looking for you! We told 'em we never heard of you!' 11 and 13. You're not the only one who can read bad polls, Josh. I am running for president in that Texas primary, and those kids are going to see me do that. And that's the only statement about my skin color I intend to make in this campaign."

~Matt Santos, "La Palabra" (S6/E18)

The HBO Special

For two decades, Wingnuts have held out for a *West Wing* reunion – with Josh Malina and other cast members lobbying for the same. Aaron Sorkin has, of course, been prodded about this many times in the press, and has consistently replied that he's not dead-set against it, but that he won't do it for its own sake; there must be some strong story idea behind such a reunion, something that would be truly new and self-justifying, to earn his green light.

Even so, we got something almost as good in the fall of 2020, just before the presidential election: *A West Wing Special to Benefit When We All Vote*, broadcast on HBO, which reunited the cast for a stage recreation of the *TWW* episode "Hartsfield's Landing" (which was about voting).

Melissa Fitzgerald & Mary McCormack related in *What's Next?* that the project was originally supposed to be a benefit for an actor's fund supporting thespians out of work, a fund depleted by the ravages of the COVID-19 pandemic. It was repurposed after the George Floyd murder, when Sorkin suggested a Zoom table read as the substance of the event, now to benefit "When We All Vote" to increase turnout in the election.

Tommy Schlamme thought that was just too small, and came back with the idea of restaging an episode as a play and filming it, "sort of in the style of a contemporary *Playhouse 90*." Sorkin loved the idea, and his thoughts turned immediately to "Hartsfield's Landing", which he considered "a valentine to voting."

Schlamme got to work staging it – it would take place in the Orpheum Theater in Los Angeles – and Sorkin started writing supplemental material. Emily Proctor had not appeared as Ainsley Hayes in that episode, but she joined the production as its narrator, reading stage instructions between acts. In addition, other cast members who hadn't been in the episode (Elizabeth Moss, Marlee Matlin) as well as outside guests (Michelle Obama, Bill Clinton, Samuel L. Jackson, Lin-Manuel Miranda) all made appearances between acts to advocate for voting.

"There was something joyous about the whole thing," said Brad Whitford in *What's Next*. "It was nostalgic and exciting and kind of awkward... a little like sleeping with your ex."

"I was struck by how easily we all fell right back into rhythm with each other," said Richard Schiff.

There was the problem of Leo McGarry, who had many lines in the episode that John Spencer, now deceased, wasn't around to perform.

"We needed someone to read John Spencer's part," Sorkin said in What's Next, "and I wanted to get someone who I knew John would respect. And that was Sterling K. Brown."

"That I was even asked was a tremendous honor," Brown said. "Honestly, that was my show... and [there were] acting crushes that I've had for years."

Anna Deavere Smith reprised NSA Nancy McNally; Melissa Fitzgerald was back as Carol Fitzpatrick; Thomas Kopache returned as Assistant Secretary of State Bobby Slattery.

Ed and Larry – Peter James Smith and William Duffy – were on hand, as were press corps members Timothy Davis-Reed (Mark O'Donnell), Mindy Seeger (Chris), and Charles Noland (Steve).

Finally, there was Snuffy Walden's gorgeous music; he played *The West Wing* theme on a classical guitar.

It wasn't exactly *new West Wing*, but it was incredibly satisfying.

~TWW~

In "Debate Camp", there is mention of a CTU – Counter Terrorist Unit. This doesn't exist in the real world; it's actually the headquarters of federal agent Jack Bauer and his colleagues in the *West Wing*-concurrent TV series 24.

Jack Bauer was played by Kieffer Sutherland; his boss in that show's first season was played by Michael O'Neill, who played Secret Service Agent Ron Butterfield on *The West Wing*.

The Best of Season Seven

"Did you know that Mozart's father believed his son to be a miracle from God? He was so convinced of this that he forced young Wolfgang to play all over Europe. His father felt it was his duty, in a world where no one believed in miracles anymore, to show them God's latest. It pretty much screwed him up for life."

~Jed Bartlet, "Mr. Frost" (S7/E4)

"Yes, a liberal Republican. What happened to them? They got run out of your party. What did liberals do that was so offensive to the Republican party? I'll tell you what they did: liberals got women the right to vote. Liberals got African-Americans the right to vote. Liberals created social security and lifted millions of elderly people out of poverty. Liberals ended segregation. Liberals passed the Civil Rights Act, the Voting Rights Act; liberals created Medicare. Liberals passed the Clean Air Act, and the Clean Water Act. What did Conservatives do? They opposed *every one* of those programs. Every one! So when you try to hurl the word 'liberal' at my feet, as if it were dirty, something to run away from, something that I should be ashamed of, it won't work, Senator! Because I will pick up that label and wear it as a badge of honor!"

~Matt Santos, "The Debate" (S7/E7)

"They want me to make sense out of all of this! And you know what, Helen? I've got nothing! Why the hell do they shoot a kid who is trying to surrender? There's some guy on the scene that says the kid was trying to put his hands up in the air. The cop couldn't have waited, like, a half a second more before he fired? And who walks around South Central with a plastic M-16? Where did this kid think he was living, Martha's Vineyard? Nobody figured out that when you live in the ghetto, you carry around something else if you don't want to get your ass blown away? That's what I've got right now. You think that's going to make anyone feel better?"

Matt Santos, "Undecideds" (S7/E8)

"You know, I find myself on days like this casting about for someone to blame. I blame the kid, he stole a car. I blame the parents. Why couldn't they teach him better? I blame the cop. Did he need to fire? I blame everyone I can think of, and I am filled with rage. And then I try and find compassion. Compassion for the people I blame. Compassion for the people I do not understand, compassion. It doesn't always work so well. I remember as a young man listening on the radio to Dr. King in 1968. He asked of us compassion, and we responded, not necessarily because we felt it, but because he convinced us that if we could find compassion, if we could express compassion, that if we could just pretend compassion, it would heal us so much more than vengeance could. And he was right: it did - but not enough. What we've learned this week is that more compassion is required of us and an even greater effort is required of us. And we are all, I think everyone of us, tired.

"We're tired of understanding, we're tired of waiting, we're tired of trying to figure out why our children are not safe and why our efforts to make them safe seem to fail! We're tired! But we must know that we have made some progress, and blame will only destroy it. Blame will breed more violence, and we have had enough of that.

"Blame will not rid our streets of crime and drugs and fear, and we have had enough of that. Blame will not strengthen our schools or our families or our workforce. Blame will rob us of those things, and we have had enough of that! And so I ask you today to dig down deep with me and find that compassion in your hearts. Because it will keep us on the road, and we will walk together and work together. And slowly, slowly, too slowly, things will get better!"

~Matt Santos, "Undecideds" (S7/E8)

"The man in that job shouldn't have to be presented with anything! It's for someone who grabs it and holds on to it, for someone who thinks the gods have conspired to bring him to this place, that destiny demands of him this service! If you don't have that kind of drive, that hubris, how in the hell are you going to make the kind of decisions that stump every other person in this country? How in the hell are you going to hold that kind of power in your hand?"

> ~Toby, to Josh, "Undecideds" (S7/E8)

"Then you will understand me when I tell you that my daughter's wedding is this afternoon and that she has been waiting for 46 minutes for me to give her away because I can't put down this damned phone until you tell me that you're not going to start World War III today! Now, for the love of God, Lian, will you give me just one half hour so I can go and walk my little girl down the aisle?"

> ~Jed Bartlet, "The Wedding" (S7/E9)

"We're both about to fall off a cliff, and I don't know what I'm going to do with the rest of my life, except I know what I don't want to do. And on Inauguration Day, you're going to be released from that glorious prison on Pennsylvania Avenue. So, if I'm going to jump off the cliff and you're going to get pushed off the cliff, why don't we hold hands on the way down?"

> ~Danny, to CJ, "Internal Displacement" (S7/E11)

"I want us to talk about what it'll mean and how we'll make it work! I want us to talk like we're gonna figure it out together! I want us to talk - because I like the sound of your voice!"

> ~Danny, to CJ, "Internal Displacement" (S7/E11)

~TWW~

"The streets of heaven are too crowded with angels tonight," Jed Bartlet says in "20 Hours in America, Pt. II", addressing the bombing at Kennison State University. Aaron Sorkin lifted that line from an actual speech – Tom Hanks' acceptance speech for the Oscar he received for *Philadelphia*.

WestWingWorld!

Note: Up to this point, we've been using WestWingWorld to refer to the television universe of the TV show. Now, as we wrap up, let's try using it to refer to a hypothetical version of an even more ambitious alternate reality – Westworld!

Welcome to WestWingWorld, the ultimate Delos adult theme park!

This unprecedented blending of state-of-the-art artificial intelligence, engineering, and dramatic innovation has created an astonishing world-within-a-world, a place where the discerning vacationer may be lost in a reverie of intellectual and philosophical extravagance, intimately celebrating the Washington of Aaron Sorkin in the company of hundreds of androids - "hosts", they are called – so life-like as to be indistinguishable from the other guests!

How does that sound? Who wouldn't want to be part of the Bartlet White House, if only for a few days – battling an opposition Congress, girded in social righteousness, surrounded by colleagues like Chief of Staff Leo McGarry, Deputy Chief Josh Lyman, Communications Director Toby Zieglar, Press Secretary C.J. Cregg, and Domestic Policy Advisor Sam Seaborn?

...To say nothing of the man himself, Jed Bartlet, First Lady Abby Bartlet, the First Daughters, body man Charlie Young, Mrs. Landingham, and the endless cast of supporting players that follow?

Who wouldn't want to relive, up close, the Mendoza Appointment? The Haffley Shutdown? The Santos Campaign? Who wouldn't want to be in the Oval Office for the Death Tax Elimination Act Veto, or Speaker Walken's swearing-in? In the Situation Room for Operation Swift Fury? In the Senate Chamber for the Stackhouse Filibuster? In the National Cathedral for Bartlet's rant against the Almighty after Mrs. Landingham's funeral?

WestWingWorld offers all of this and more! The characters of *The West Wing* come to life in full-scale replicas of the White House, the Mall, Capitol Hill and select sections of Georgetown. More than 140 narratives are available; for those who know all the words of every episode, it's possible to step into the role of any major character, including the president – or you can participate improvisationally as an extra, adding your own accents to Sorkin's beloved stories.

Have you ever dreamed of being Presidents Carter, Clinton and JFK all rolled into one? Then be Josiah Barlet, Nobel Prize-winning ex-governor of New Hampshire, the shortest president since Truman – brilliant, yet accessible; erudite, yet folksy – and try out that Oval Office chair! Get Roberto Mendoza confirmed to the Supreme Court! Holler for Mrs. Landingham! Refuse Toby's resignations! Broker peace between Israel and Palestine! Fail to disclose your multiple sclerosis! All in a day's work.

Or be the president's best friend, the ultra-competent Leo: run the country, inspire your staff, urge the president to roll up his sleeves! Yank the vice president's chain! Endure public humiliation over your past substance abuse; dance with women six inches taller than you; square off against Lord John Marbury; admonish the Religious Right! Get taken out for a walk by a Congressional committee! Relive your heart attack in the Birnam Woods!

Are you dour, joyless, self-righteous, and even smarter than the president himself? Then you'll enjoy being Toby Zieglar, identifying Walter Hufnagle's overcoat on the Mall; refusing pie from ex-wife Andy by the Potomac, or providing her with sperm for in vitro fertilization; getting up in the president's face, oh, just about any time; or leaking the existence of a classified military space shuttle to Greg Brock of the *New York Times*. Or just save social security!

What woman wouldn't love to be C.J. Gregg for a while? Be the press secretary presidents dream of! Be wittier and quicker on your feet than the entire White House press corps combined; tease Danny Concannon; be stunning in off-the-rack dresses; be *really great* in bed! Then step into the role of Chief of Staff, under the worst of circumstances, leapfrogging all of your male colleagues, without missing a beat!

If you're too arrogant to live and too sexy for your shirt, you'll do well as Josh Lyman – Leo's right hand, supervisor of 1,100 West Wing staffers, and the 101st senator. Bring home the Family Wellness Act; steal the First Lady's $12 million immunization education fund; thwart your activist girlfriend Amy by hiring her boss; take a bullet in the chest and come up swinging! Or work his other side, and diss Mary Marsh on national television; lean on Senator Carrick so hard that he turns Republican; take Donna for granted until she quits and joins the Russell campaign.

And how 'bout that Donna, right? You could *be* her, fighting the good fight alongside Josh every day, building up the know-how and skills that will eventually make *you* a chief of staff yourself, to the next FLOTUS! Live it all, from your brazen on-boarding in the first campaign, to your missile-silo-under-the-Eisenhower-putting-green gaffe, to the Gaza mission and your near-death in the suburban - and your bittersweet moments with Irish photojournalist Colin Ayres.

And if you're cool as all hell but don't need to flaunt it, you'll do well as Charlie Young, the president's body man – smarter than Josh and Sam and C.J. put together, loved like a son by the president (don't miss the Paul Revere's Knife Scene!), and loved like a lover by his youngest daughter. You'll wake the president at ungodly hours; watch for symptoms of M.S.; bust Zoey's sexual harassers in a Georgetown bar; have the president himself do your tax return! Proudly refuse immunity in the M.S. cover-up investigation - or experience the existential horror of realizing that it was you, not the president, that the shooters at Roslyn were gunning for.

And, of course, it wouldn't be the West Wing without Sam. You can be the earnest, talented deputy communications director, outshining even the president in your optimism, balancing out that moody Toby with your youthful pluck and constant good spirits. Land the State of the Union! Spar with Ainsley Hayes! Walk out of Gage Whitney on the spur of the moment, just from a glance at Josh's bad poker face; sit with Nancy McNally in the Sit Room, defending Daniel Galt; leak the Ritchie campaign's nasty opposition video by mistake, jeopardizing your boss's re-elect; run for Congress to comfort a hometown widow!

It's not just the characters that make WestWingWorld special; it's the unique experience of living among androids that look and feel and act as real as you yourself.

Are you action-oriented? Do bombs, bullets and mayhem get your engine running? Well, that's no problem, because the hosts of WestWingWorld are just machines – you aren't breaking any laws or truly committing any moral breach! You won't *really* be assassinating Abdul Sharif; you won't *really* be blowing up four high-rated military targets in Syria; when you blow away the shooters in the window at Roslyn, they won't *really* die!

And think of the off-script possibilities: wouldn't it be great to be Secret Service agent Simon Donovan, walk into that convenience store and, instead of being killed, take down both robbers, then do C.J. all night long?

Yes, if you've got some mojo that needs indulging, WestWingWorld hosts are *fully functional*, able to cater to the most intimate desires of guests – completely consequence-free, because they're just robots! You can be Sam, and accidentally sleep with a prostitute; be the First Lady, and take the president's temperature "recreationally"; experience a night of shame with the philandering John Hoynes; step out of Charlie Young's shoes, and into First Daughter Zoey's bedroom after hours (or vice versa), right under the president's nose!

Or change *West Wing* history in this domain as well – be Josh, having a campaign fling with Donna on the first campaign, rather than the last; or be Sam, and get it on with Leo's daughter Mallory at the Kennedy Center; be C.J., and decide you no longer have a problem with the press secretary dating a reporter.

Just $40,000 a day is all it takes to bring the imaginary world of Aaron Sorkin's *West Wing* to life – to experience the living, breathing characters we've all loved these many years, to make yourself part of the action! Call or visit our website today, and get started on the greatest, most mentally stimulating vacation of your life!

UPDATE: WestWingWorld will be closing indefinitely, pending extensive review and revision of its revenue model. Due to numerous media revelations of the recent string of guest bankruptcies, foreclosures, exorbitant credit card debt and exhausted retirement accounts, a number of fraud investigations at both federal and state levels have been initiated.

Park administrators have assured the public and press that no malfeasance has occurred, that many guests truly have been spending all that they have, free of coercion or undue influence, to continue being in the park, and have issued the following statement from the Delos public relations office:

"WestWingWorld's inquiry into the recent financial difficulties of its most frequent guests has included extensive exit surveys, compiling their reactions to the narratives in which they have participated. The conclusion of our counselors, as well as outside consultants, is uniform: once guests experience truly good government, immersed in a world of competent, intelligent, committed and principled public servants who forego more comfortable and lucrative lives in order to do some real good – a world where they truly matter, and the greater good ultimately prevails over craven politics and the cynicism of partisanship - they simply cannot bring themselves to ever leave."

If you enjoyed
*What's Next? The West Wing Big Book
of Superfan Fun,*
leave a review on Amazon.com!

See more of
the *What's Next?* series
on the following pages...

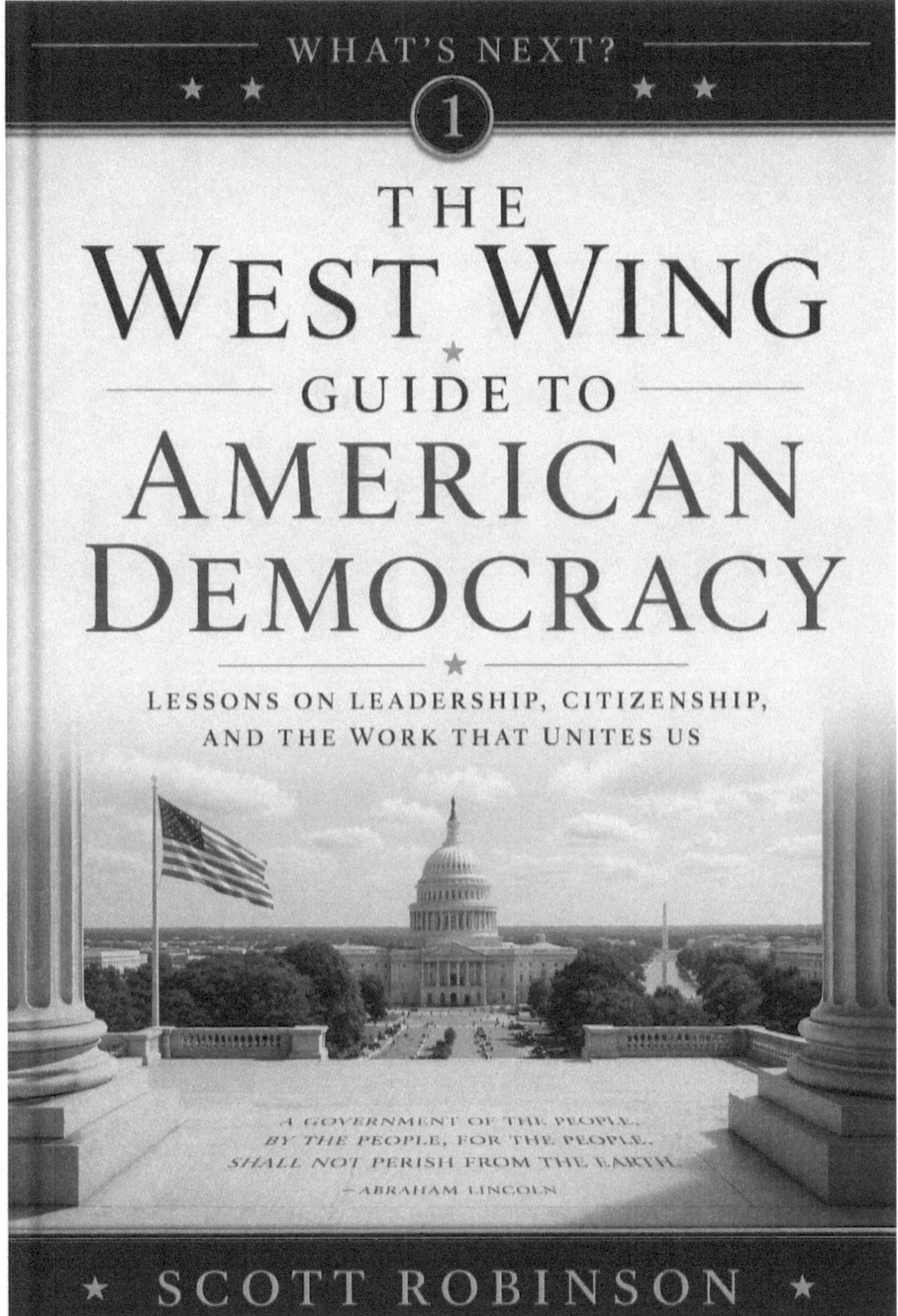
WHAT'S NEXT?
1
THE
WEST WING
GUIDE TO
AMERICAN
DEMOCRACY
LESSONS ON LEADERSHIP, CITIZENSHIP,
AND THE WORK THAT UNITES US
A GOVERNMENT OF THE PEOPLE,
BY THE PEOPLE, FOR THE PEOPLE,
SHALL NOT PERISH FROM THE EARTH.
—ABRAHAM LINCOLN
SCOTT ROBINSON

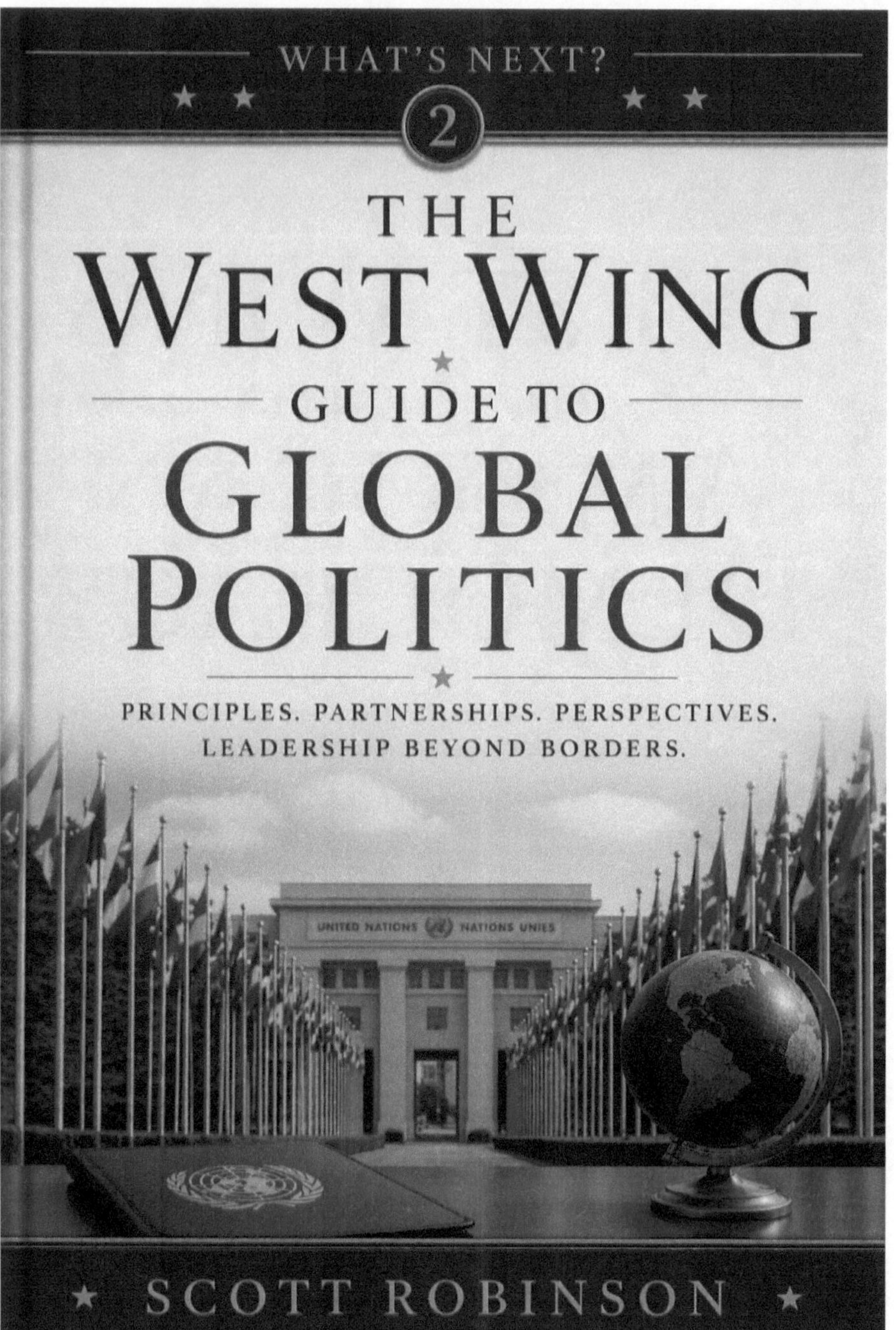
WHAT'S NEXT?
2
THE
WEST WING
GUIDE TO
GLOBAL
POLITICS
PRINCIPLES. PARTNERSHIPS. PERSPECTIVES.
LEADERSHIP BEYOND BORDERS.
UNITED NATIONS · NATIONS UNIES
★ SCOTT ROBINSON ★

WHAT'S NEXT?
3
THE
WEST WING
ULTIMATE
SUPERFAN
TRIVIA CHALLENGE!
★ TRIVIA QUIZZES FROM ALL 7 SEASONS ★
QUESTION:
What vegetable does
President Bartlet dislike?
A. Spinach
B. Cabbage
C. Green Beans
D. Corn
THE
WEST WING
SCOTT ROBINSON

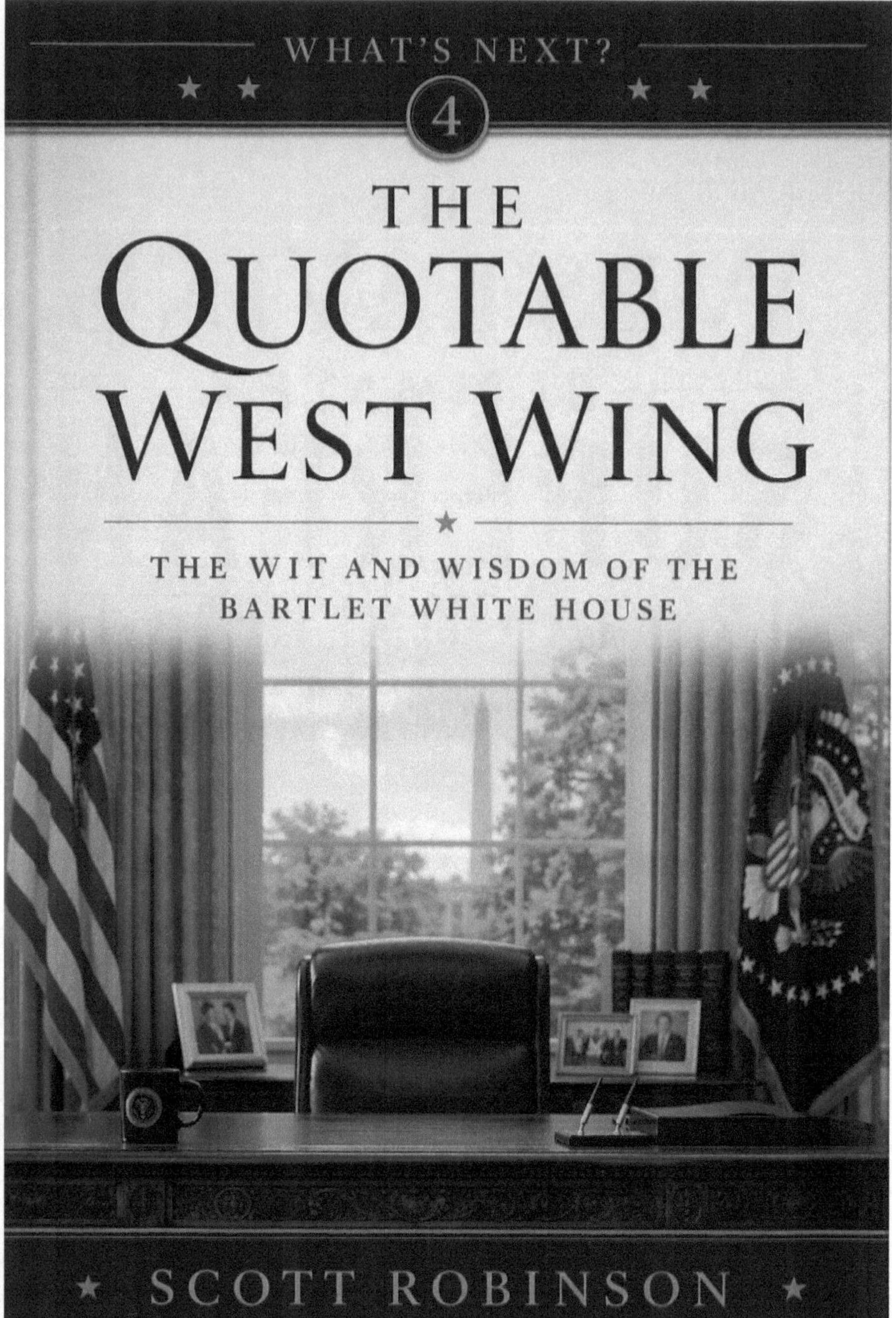
WHAT'S NEXT?
4
THE
QUOTABLE
WEST WING
THE WIT AND WISDOM OF THE
BARTLET WHITE HOUSE
SCOTT ROBINSON

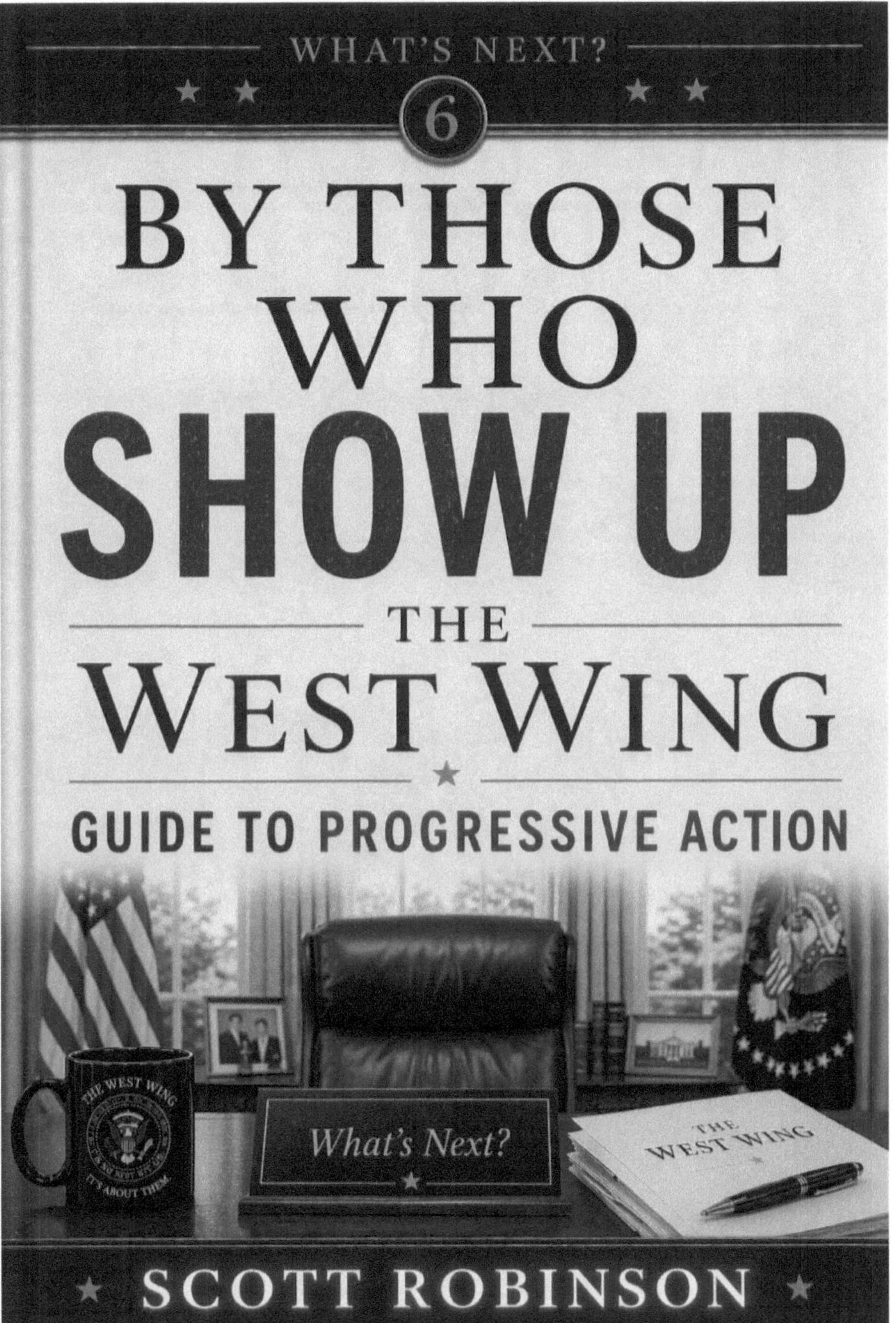
WHAT'S NEXT?
6
BY THOSE WHO SHOW UP
THE WEST WING
GUIDE TO PROGRESSIVE ACTION
What's Next?
THE WEST WING
SCOTT ROBINSON

RED BRAINS,
BLUE BRAINS
The Psychology of MAGA
Scott Robinson

RED BRAINS, BLUE BRAINS
Authoritarian We Will Go!
Scott Robinson

MILLENNIUM 7
7
THEY LONG TO
END DEMOCRACY
MINORITY RULE ON THE MARCH
POWER OVER PEOPLE
TRADITION OVER TRUTH
CONTROL OVER FREEDOM
PRIVILEGE OVER EQUALITY
THE THREAT IS NOT LOUD.
IT IS ORGANIZED.
SCOTT ROBINSON
7

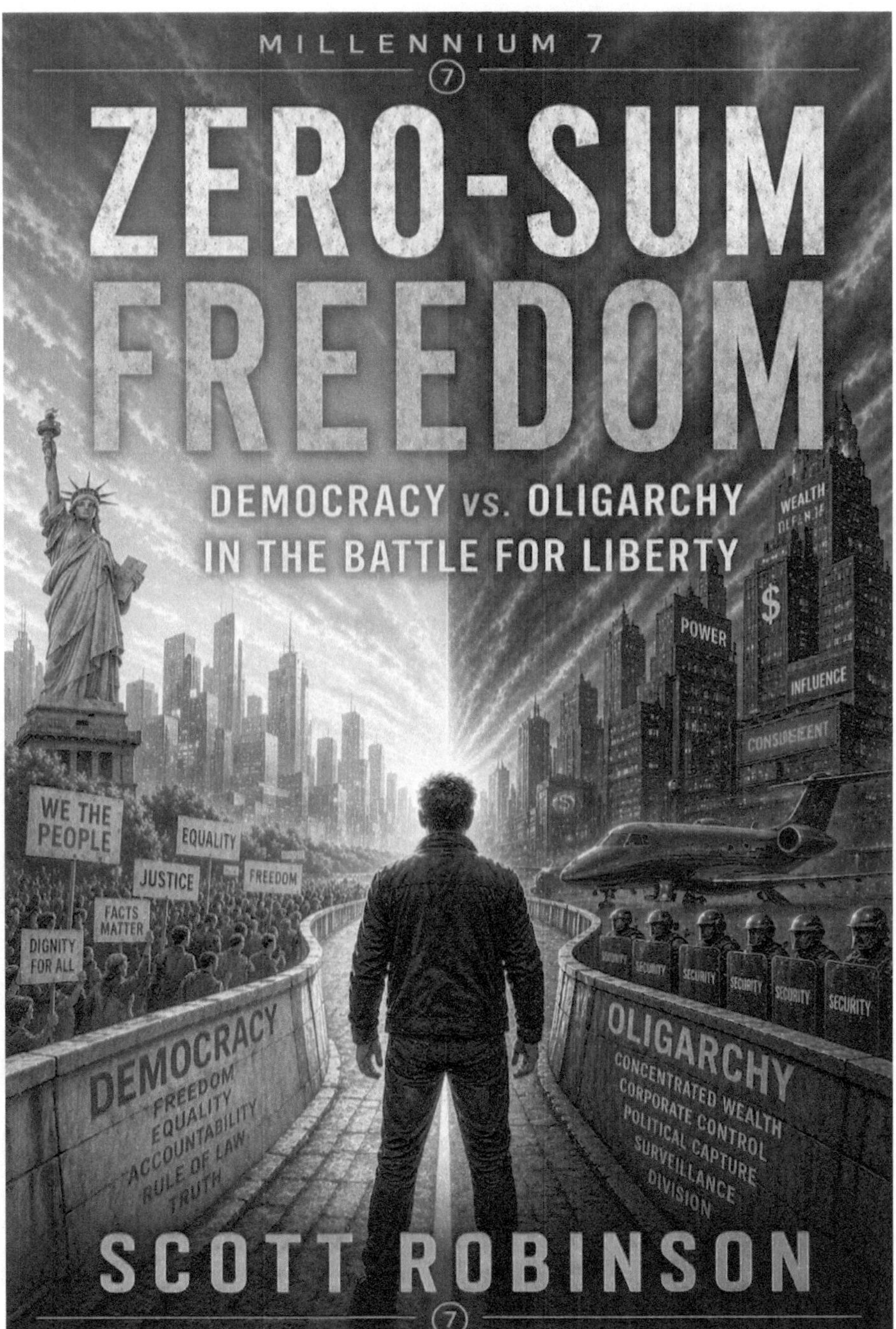
MILLENNIUM 7
7
ZERO-SUM
FREEDOM
DEMOCRACY vs. OLIGARCHY
IN THE BATTLE FOR LIBERTY
WEALTH
POWER
$
INFLUENCE
WE THE
PEOPLE
EQUALITY
JUSTICE
FREEDOM
FACTS
MATTER
DIGNITY
FOR ALL
SECURITY
SECURITY
SECURITY
SECURITY
SECURITY
SECURITY
DEMOCRACY
FREEDOM
EQUALITY
ACCOUNTABILITY
RULE OF LAW
TRUTH
OLIGARCHY
CONCENTRATED WEALTH
CORPORATE CONTROL
POLITICAL CAPTURE
SURVEILLANCE
DIVISION
SCOTT ROBINSON
7

EXPLORING THE ETHICS OF THE FINAL FRONTIER

STAR TREK AND HUMANISM

Living by the Star Trek Ethos in a Troubled World

SCOTT ROBINSON

BOLDLY GOING — BOOK #1

*What would it take to actually build
the world Star Trek imagined?*

PLURIBUS
JOY & DREAD
IN THE BENEVOLENT MACHINE
SCOTT ROBINSON

Wingnut Superfan Resources

Here are some excellent Wingnut websites...

https://westwing.fandom.com/wiki/West_Wing_Wiki

http://www.westwingtranscripts.com/search.php

https://transcripts.foreverdreaming.org/viewforum.php?f=923

http://westwing.bewarne.com/default.html

and, of course,

http://thewestwingweekly.com

Bibliography / Recommended Reading

Books

Considering Aaron Sorkin: Essays on the Politics, Poetics and Sleight of Hand in the Films and Television Series, Thomas Fahy. McFarland, 2009.

Mr. Sorkin Goes to Washington: Shaping the President on Television's The West Wing, Melissa Crawley. McFarland, 2009.

The Quotable West Wing, Scott Robinson. Paleos Media, 2024.

The West Wing: The American Presidency as Television Drama, Peter C. Rollins, John E. O'Connor. Syracuse University Press, 2003.

The West Wing Guide to American Democracy, Scott Robinson. Paleos Media, 2023.

The West Wing Guide to Global Politics, Scott Robinson. Paleos Media, 2024.

The West Wing Ultimate Superfan Trivia Challenge!, Scott Robinson. Paleos Media, 2024.

What's Next? A Backstage Pass to The West Wing, Its Cast and Crew, and Its Enduring Legacy of Service, Melissa Fitzgerald & Mary McCormack. Dutton, 2024.

Internet

https://digitalcommons.bucknell.edu/cgi/viewcontent.cgi?article=1498&context=honors_theses

https://americanpopularculture.com/journal/articles/fall_2009/kim.htm

https://www.sutori.com/en/story/leadership-in-the-west-wing--s1AeRHDzcJABgQVyk12nqXjE

https://harvardpolitics.com/waiting-for-bartlet/

https://prospect.org/article/case-for-jed-bartlet/

https://networkforpubliceducation.org/blog-content/john-thompson-lessons-from-the-west-wing

https://archive.thinkprogress.org/josiah-bartlet-was-a-mediocre-president-f1532df9185e

ABOUT THE AUTHOR

Scott Robinson is an artificial intelligence designer, social scientist, public speaker and musician, and serves as Director of Technology and Content for the non-profit Humanity Prime. He has been published in *Rolling Stone* and *The Wall Street Journal*. He can be found at

scottrobinsonwriter@gmail.com